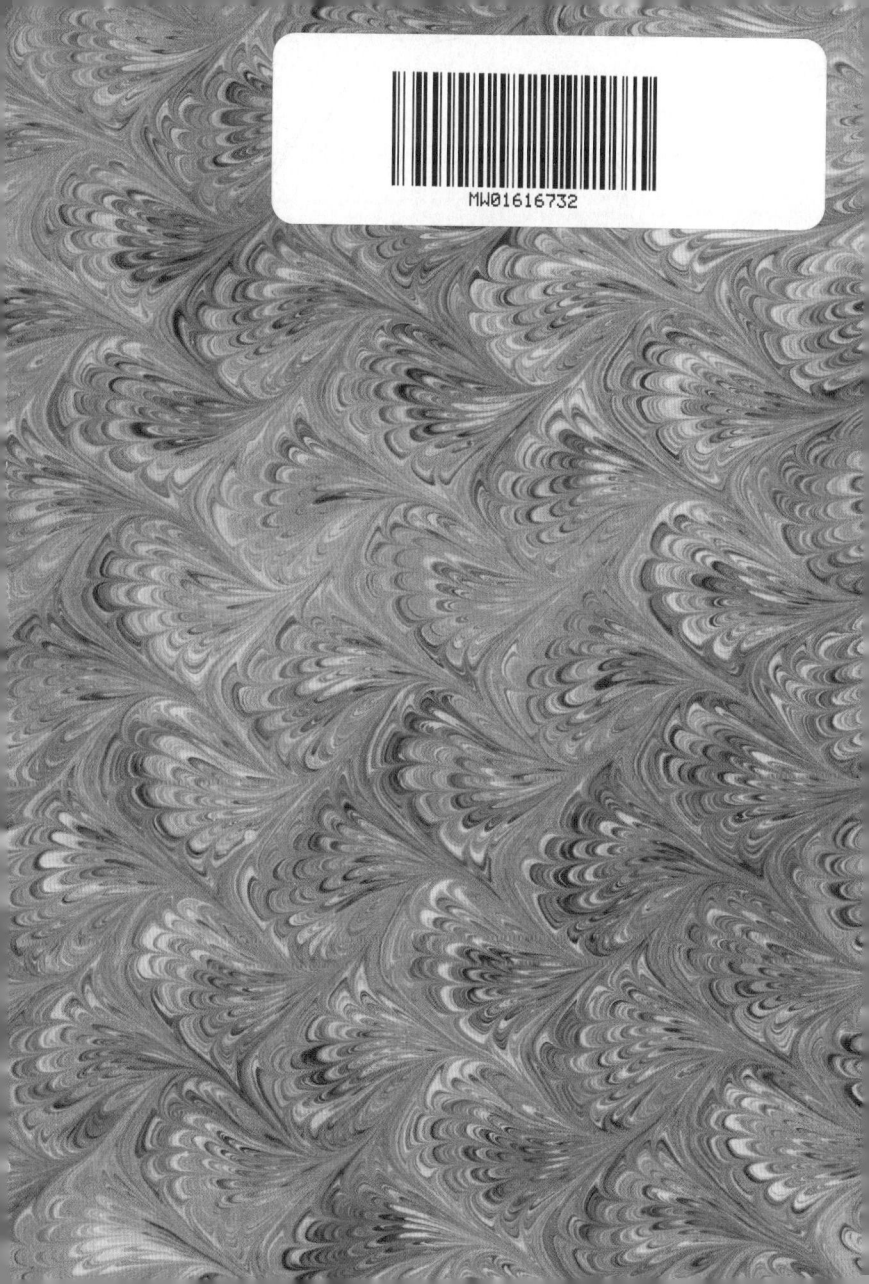

MW01616732

THE HEAVENLY GIFT

The Ancient Art of Liturgical Bread-Making

Publisher's Cataloging-In-Publication Data

Names: Stravrou-Michalski, Dimitra, author. | Stamatis, Stravroula, author.
| Monos, Michael, translator, author.

Title:The heavenly gift : the ancient art of liturgical bread-making / Dimitra Stravrou-Michalski [and] Stravroula Stamatis ; translated and adapted by Ref. Protopresbyter Michael G. Monos.

Other titles: Prosforo kai Artos. English

Description: [First English edition]. | [Columbia, Missouri] : Newrome Press, [2023] | First published in Greek as: Prosforo kai Artos. Athens, Greece : Athos Publications, 2018. | Includes bibliographical references.

Identifiers: ISBN: 978-1-957662-13-8

Subjects: LCSH: Bread--Religious aspects--Christianity. | Cooking (Bread)--History. | Bread stamps (Liturgical objects)--History. | Orthodox Eastern Church--Liturgical objects.

Classification: LCC: BV825.52 .P7613 2023 | DDC: 234/.16--dc23

DIMITRA STAVROU-MICHALSKI

STAVROULA STAMATIS

THE HEAVENLY GIFT

The Ancient Art of Liturgical Bread-Making

Translated and Adapted by

REV. PROTOPRESBYTER MICHAEL G. MONOS

Newrome
PRESS

ĪC ō X̄C
Ō N

THE LIFE GIVER

YOU WILL KNOW THE TRUTH, AND THE TRUTH WILL SET YOU FREE!

"Amen, amen, I tell you; the one who believes in Me has eternal life. I am the bread of life! Your ancestors ate the manna in the wilderness, and they died. This is the bread which comes down out of Heaven. Its purpose is that anyone may eat of it and not die. I am the living bread which came down out of Heaven. Anyone who eats of this bread will live forever! Yes, the bread which I will give for the life of the world is My flesh."

John 6:47-51

For I received from the Lord what also I delivered to you, that the Lord Jesus, on the night in which He was betrayed, took bread. When He had given thanks, He broke it, and said, "Take, eat. This is My body, which is broken for you. Do this in memory of Me." Likewise, He also took the cup, after supper, saying, "This cup is the new covenant in My Blood. Do this, as often as you drink, in memory of Me." For as often as you eat this bread and drink this cup, you proclaim the Lord's death until He comes.

1 Cor. 11:23-26

Before every Divine Liturgy, the priest celebrates the Service of Preparation. During this service, loaves of bread are prepared by the faithful and subdivided by the priest at the Table of Preparation. The first piece excised from the loaf is the Lamb, which will become the Body of our Lord and Savior Jesus Christ. Following this, the priest continues to excise the portions for the Most Holy Theotokos, the holy Angels, the Saints, and, lastly, the faithful, both the living and the departed. These various pieces are placed around the Lamb on the holy diskarion.

Behold—the entire Church is represented on the diskarion! Our Lord, the Panagia, the honorable Forerunner, the Prophets, Apostles, Martyrs, Ascetics, Righteous, all the Saints, form a choir with us, the fallen and humble. Here we see the fellowship of the living and the departed, of saints and sinners, of God with mankind! This is the Orthodox Church of Christ!

—Saint John of Kronstadt

Preface

Rev. Protopresbyter Michael G. Monos

There is a unique joy that comes from giving—for both the giver and the receiver. Holy Scripture abounds with examples of human persons making offerings to God—not, of course, because God needs material things. Rather, such offerings were made out of devotion, gratitude, love, and for justice. Fundamentally, in making any offering to God we follow the example of God Himself who made the most sublime offering of His Son to us for our eternal salvation.

Preparing and offering prosphoro for the celebration of the Immaculate Mysteries is a joy and a unique privilege for the faithful Orthodox Christian. It is, essentially, a love-act of thanksgiving toward God and one's fellow brothers and sisters in Christ, both living and reposed. It makes possible the most transcendent of all worshipful acts, the divine transformation of common earthly elements into the Heavenly Gift—the very Body and Blood of our Lord, God, and Savior Jesus Christ, for health of soul and body and the remission of sins unto eternal life. "If union with God is the ultimate goal of the Christian's spiritual life . . . nowhere else is such an intimate union accomplished than through the reception of the Body and Blood of Christ."[1]

This English edition of Πρόσφορο καὶ Ἄρτος has been retranslated, updated, and adapted for use in an American kitchen. The most significant changes appear in chapter two, The Preparation of Prosphoro and Artoclasia Bread.[2] The reasons for the present adaptation are simple: cooking tools, measurements, and available ingredients differ from place to place. While globalization brings sameness in many areas of life, foodstuffs and kitchens in Europe are plainly different than in America. An individual could certainly

1. George Dokos, *Made for Union: The Sacramental Spirituality of St. Nikodemos of the Holy Mountain* (Columbia, Missouri: Newrome Press, 2020), 138.

2. The editor would like to stress that this adaptation in no way intends to diminish the original Greek edition and its particular methodology. However, since we hope to encourage Orthodox Christians in the west to participate in this ancient tradition, then sensible adjustments to approach, which are founded upon their particular context, needed to be made.

attempt to make adjustments and test results through trial and error, but this can be a difficult and frustrating process, especially considering that a single prosphoro takes more than 10 hours to prepare, rise, and bake! Baking itself is an art, and even experienced bakers encounter failures in the kitchen. With that in mind, this edition makes specific recommendations to assist the baker in the process. It is hoped that these recommendations make the process less intimidating.

The adapted process, as described in this edition, has been thoroughly tested in a home kitchen on consumer-grade equipment. The suggested ingredients, tools, and bakeware have all been used during the assembly of this edition. None of the companies mentioned in this book have sponsored its publication. Thus the various recommendations are solely the result of firsthand experience in the preparation of many, many prosphora. Furthermore, none of the prosphora photographs included in this edition have been retouched to enhance their appearance.

Finally, as the authors of the original Greek edition state, this book is a collective effort that builds on the experiences and efforts of many people. This is not the work of a single editor / translator, but a work of and for the Church itself, for the glory of God!

Contents

CHAPTER FOUR

Prosphora, Seals, and Bread from Ancient to Modern

CHAPTER FIVE

Everyday Stories

PHOTOGRAPHIC AIDS

Introduction

a. Bread, Daily Bread, and the Bread of Life

Every day, for more than two thousand years, count-less Christians have entreated God, the Creator of the universe, when reciting the Lord's Prayer. Like lit-tle children, we ask our heavenly Father to "Give us this day our daily bread" (Matt. 6:11), following the in-struction of our Lord Jesus Christ to the Apostles. This prayer is slightly different in the words of Saint Luke the Evangelist: "Give us day by day our daily bread" (Luke 11:3). What exactly are we asking from God with this supplication? Are we simply asking Him to give us a portion of bread? Or perhaps we are asking for some-thing more, which is nevertheless material? Or maybe our fundamental request is in fact the sum of every spiritual and material good—the immaterial, indescribable, and eternal, together with what is tangible, perceptible, and transient. In other words, perhaps we are asking for nothing less than the bounties of both earth and Heaven!

There is no doubt that our prayerful supplication is a confession of faith that God, as a compassionate Father, providentially cares for His creatures. And while we cannot fully comprehend the magnitude of God's power and His providential care of creation, our entreaty expresses a wholehearted desire to live in communion with Him. The words of the prayer, "Our Father . . . our daily bread . . ." in the first-person plural reveals that we are not alone in this relationship. The "our" does not mean a single couple, family, city, or even one country, but rather refers to the entire human race. The supplication for "bread" is in truth an entreaty for fellowship with God and our brethren. This communion, which existed when the world was created, was broken on account of mankind's challenge to the loving Creator's divine commandments. Man misused his freedom, and ultimately lost the divine fellowship that he once enjoyed. Paradise, a source of divine joy, was exchanged for the loneliness of the wilderness and enslavement to the passions.

However, our heavenly Father had already planned to restore what had been lost in the Garden through the sacrificial offering of His own Son on the Cross, and thereby open the gates of Paradise. Our Savior's crucified Body is tangible proof of God's authentic love for us, a love "obedient to the point of death, even death on the Cross!" (Phil. 2:8).

Before our Lord was crucified, He entrusted the mystery of the Divine Eucharist to His disciples, saying, "Take, eat; this is My Body" (Matt. 26:26), and gave them a portion of sanctified bread. He then said, "Drink [from] it all of you, for this is My Blood" (Matt. 26:27-28), and gave them a portion of sanctified wine. The sanctified bread of the Divine Eucharist is the Body of Christ, and the sanctified wine is the Blood of Christ. The special eucharistic bread, prepared and provided to priests and the Church by the faithful, is called *prosphoro,*[1] which means "that which is offered." The bread of offering is made from flour; the flour in turn is made from wheat; the wheat is made from seed; and the seed itself is a gift from God to gladden the heart of mankind and to sustain him. Indeed, ev-

---

1   The plural form is *prosphora.*

erything that we cultivate, eat, and possess is a divine benefaction! Whenever a person prepares and brings the eucharistic bread to his priest or church, he makes a small offering back to God from the wealth of His infinite goodness—the source of our breath, food, life, joy, and sanctification: "Your own of Your own, we offer unto You in all and for all!" (Divine Liturgy).

The Holy Spirit transforms this prosphoro, offered in love and gratitude, into the Body of Christ, the Bread of Life, which is "the food for the whole world" (Prayer of the Proskomide). This bread fully satiates the spiritually hungry and grants true knowledge and authentic liberty.

4

True knowledge is the experience of divine love.

Authentic liberty is the annihilation of death, which casts out the fear of material deprivation.

"I am the Bread of Life!" (John 6:35).

b. The Temptation of Materiality and Fasting

By nature, matter itself is not intermingled with sin. Everything that God created was made "very good" (Gen. 1:31). However, dependence upon or an improper attachment to matter is sinful. Quite simply, such an attitude of life lays waste to our personal freedom, be-

cause it overturns the natural order of things by placing creation above the Creator. The way of holiness—
the way of Christ—understands that the whole, which
is God, is more than the sum of its parts. Sometimes
we mistakenly allow the various dimensions of daily
living to consume us and, in so doing, we forget Christ.
Nothing on the road of life should take precedence
over our relationship with the Creator and Benefactor
of all things.

Before the Lord began His public ministry, He departed into the wilderness and fasted for forty days.
There, in the Judean desert, on the Mount of Temptation, the devil attempted to seduce our Lord to sin,
saying, "'If You are the Son of God, command that
these stones become bread.' But Jesus answered, 'It is
written: One shall not live by bread alone, but by every word that comes out of the mouth of God!'" (Matt.
4:3-4).

The precious Body and Blood of Christ—a piece
of prosphoro soaked in sweet wine—that the faithful
receive in the Divine Eucharist is preceded by a period of fasting. This abstinence allows each believer
to emulate, if only in a small way, our Lord's sojourn
in the desert and His revelation to the wicked devil

on the Mount of Temptation, "'Man shall not live by bread alone, but by every word that proceeds out of the mouth of God'" (Luke 4:4). The fast is not merely material—abstinence from certain foods—but also spiritual. "Brethren, let us fast bodily and spiritually" (Aposticha of Lamplighting, Tuesday, Second Week of Great Lent). Our spiritual fasting invites us to abandon every unseemly attachment, to feed the hungry, to aid the homeless, to comfort the sorrowful, to be exceedingly patient with our brethren, and to manage our daily living with humility so that we might receive divine mercy.

c. Our Dear Mother, the Heavenly Manna, and the House of Bread

Prosphoro is brought to the Church as an offering to be sanctified and transformed into the Body of Christ; it also symbolizes our Lord's all-holy Mother. The round shape of the loaf symbolizes her holy womb, in which she carried the Christ. As Joachim and Anna offered their daughter to God who was received into sacred precincts of the Temple, so too do we offer the prosphoro to become the Body of Christ.

The Bread of Offering is also related to the heavenly manna, the wondrous food that nourished the Israelites during their journey in the wilderness, and the heavenly food that an Angel of the Lord provided for the sustenance of the Most-holy Theotokos while she dwelt in the Holy of Holies of the Temple.

We could say that the prosphoro transports us to ancient Bethlehem—the "House of Bread"—where our Lord, the true Bread of Life, was born in the flesh.

On every day permissible, the Divine Liturgy is celebrated in holy temples all over the earth. In those sacred places, where two or three gather "in His name," this most sublime mystery of the Church unfolds—the transformation of the bread and wine into the precious Body and Blood of our Lord and Savior Jesus Christ through the power of the Holy Spirit. The preparation and offering of the prosphoro is our way of thanking God for His abiding love, providential care, and countless wonders—known and unknown, seen and unseen.

7

Prosphoro and the Divine Liturgy

CHAPTER ONE

a. The Bread of Offering as Preparation

In Greek, the prosphoro is often called *leitouryiá* (liturgy). Indeed, the preparation of the Divine Liturgy begins with the kneading of the prosphoro, from which will be excised the Lamb (the central portion that will become the Body of Christ), and those portions for the Mother of God, the holy Angels, the Saints, and the antidoron.[1] This important ecclesiastical act of service for the Church has been a blessing to many Christians,

---

1. *Antidoron*, which comes from the Greek, ἀντὶ (instead) + δῶρον (gift), means "Instead of the Gift," and was traditionally distributed to those Christians who, for one reason or another, were unable or unprepared to receive Holy Communion.

and most especially to women who have had a primary role in the preparation of the Bread of Offering in parish churches.

In ancient times, the housewife readied herself for the preparation of the prosphoro in what resembled a sacred rite. As a certain elderly housewife in the Dodecanese told the authors: "Before we knead and bake the Bread of Offering, we must bathe, dress in clean clothing, and put on a new apron. Then we pull back our hair and cover our head with a clean white scarf. Furthermore, we never bake prosphoro during our menstrual period." In other words, she prepared herself for the leitouryiá with an awareness of the sacred character of the work. "It was as if they were donning a priestly stole," explains Archimandrite Doistheos in the *Orthodox Pilgrim's Guide*.

The selection of ingredients for the baking must be chosen with extreme care. For example, the flour must be pure sifted wheat. Additionally, the tools and bakeware used must be clean, and if possible, reserved for this purpose alone. The prep area must also be clean and orderly. And finally, the one preparing the offering should be spiritually clean through fasting, prayer, and self-restraint.

The task of preparing the Bread of Offering is not uniquely intended for one sex—both women and men are able to share in this honorable service to Christ's holy Church, so long as they approach their service to the Church with gratitude and joy. Indeed, whether a person is a member of the clergy or the laity, everything that they do should be done for the Lord.

b. From Hearth to Church

How and when we bring our offering to the church is important. When we make our offering, we should conduct ourselves with quiet humility, never drawing attention to ourselves. The prosphoro must be delivered at an appropriate time—before or after the celebration of a divine service. Ideally, the prosphoro should be delivered at Vespers on the evening before it is needed. If the Service of Vespers is not scheduled to be celebrated, then we must arrive before the Service of Orthros has begun.

11

At the church, the prosphoro should be given to one of the adult altar servers, or to the priest himself, wrapped in a clean towel or placed in a plastic food storage bag, such as a Ziploc bag. With our offering we include a list of the names of living and reposed

Orthodox Christians whom we ask the priest to commemorate during the Service of the Preparation.[2] This is an act of love—to purposefully participate in bringing about a spiritual communion between the person commemorated and our Lord. We should remember to include not only friends and family, but also those who have wronged, grieved, or otherwise harmed us, since this contributes to our forgiveness of their transgressions against us and our reconciliation with them. Furthermore, we should be careful to write our commemoration lists legibly, so that they can be easily read by the priest.

The process of preparing prosphoro teaches us patience, and that everything in life passes through a period of maturation. The Orthodox Church chooses to work with fermented[3] products (bread and wine) rather than unfermented ones. This teaches us something important about life: spiritual growth requires patience, careful consideration, and discernment.

---

2. Commemoration lists should include just the full first baptismal/chrismation name of Orthodox Christians. We should not use nicknames or shorthand such as "The Smith Family."

3. Or, "leavened" products.

c. The Table of Preparation, the Service of Preparation, the Offering, and Holy Communion

The Service of Preparation is performed prior to the celebration of the Divine Liturgy at a place in the church called the *Prothesis* (Table of Preparation).[4] The prothesis is an area at the north end of the sanctuary, most often set within a small apse. During the rite, the priest excises portions from one or more prosphora and places them on the diskarion.[5] The diskarion symbolizes the Lord's manger, His bier, Heaven, and the whole universe.

13

A ceremonial knife called the *holy lance* is used to excise portions from the prosphoro. This lance symbolizes the spear used by the Roman soldier to pierce Christ's holy Body on the Cross. The priest excises the Lamb—the central portion—from the first prosphoro, which is stamped with a Cross and the inscrip-

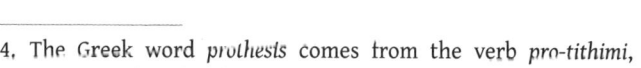

4. The Greek word *prothesis* comes from the verb *pro-tithimi*, meaning "to place before."

5. Also called the *paten*. The *diskarion* is a small round metal disk with a stemmed base on which is placed the Lamb, which is to be consecrated as well as the other portions that are taken out from the Bread of Offering. Oftentimes the diskarion has an engraving of the Theotokos.

tion ΙΣ ΧΣ ΝΙ ΚΑ (an abbreviation for Ἰησοῦς Χριστὸς νικᾷ, "Jesus Christ Conquers"). After he removes it, the priest makes two deep vertical cuts on the underside of the Lamb, saying, "The Lamb of God who takes away the sins of the world is sacrificed for the life and salvation of the world . . . When you were crucified, O Christ, the tyranny of the devil was destroyed; the power of the enemy was crushed. For it was not an angel of a man who saved us, O Lord, but You. Glory be to You!" (Service of Preparation). The priest then places the Lamb on the diskarion. Next, the priest pierces the seal of the Lamb where the letters ΙΣ are inscribed while saying, "One of the soldiers pierced His side and immediately there came forth blood and water, and he who has seen it has borne witness and his testimony is true." And then the priest pours wine and water into the holy Chalice, which will become the Blood of Christ.

If there are other prosphora, the priest will use those for the other portions; however, if there is only one, he will complete the rite of preparation with that one prosphoro. The next piece to be excised is the portion for the Theotokos, which is placed to the right of the Lamb, while to the left the priest places the portions for the Angels and the Saints. The particles excised for the living and the reposed are placed either in front of the Lamb or on the right and left under the other portions. A metal liturgical item called the "star" or "asterisk," which symbolizes the star of Bethlehem, is placed over the Lamb on the diskarion. The star prevents the veil from touching the Lamb. After the Chalice is veiled, both are covered with a larger veil called the *aeras*, which symbolizes the winding sheet that Joseph of Arimathea used to enshroud the dead Body of our Lord. The covered precious Gifts remain on the Table of Preparation until the Great Entrance, which is a series of hymns, prayers, and actions that are performed when the precious Gifts are transferred to the Holy Table.

The Great Entrance, according to the Fathers of the Church, symbolizes our Lord's entry into Jerusalem,

His martyric road to Golgotha and the Cross, and His entombment. The characteristic hymn of this part of the Divine Liturgy is called the Cherubic Hymn, which encourages the faithful to "lay aside all earthly cares" in order to receive "the King of all." During the transfer of the unconsecrated precious Gifts, the sacred vessels are carried from the Table of Preparation into the nave of the temple through the midst of the faithful[6] and finally placed on the Holy Table.

During the recitation of the Symbol of Faith, the aeras is lifted above and waved over the precious Gifts by the celebrant(s). This action signifies the presence of the Holy Spirit. The Holy Anaphora, which means an "offering up," follows with the angelic exhortation, "Let us stand well, let us stand with fear." After this, the priest exclaims, "The grace of our Lord Jesus Christ, the love of God the Father, and the communion of the Holy Spirit be with you all." After this blessing the choir responds, "And with your spirit," signifying that the faithful present for this Liturgy join together with the officiants in its celebration. Having given

16

---

6. During the Liturgy of the Presanctified Gifts, the priest actually carries the Body and Blood of Christ in procession, since they were consecrated at the Divine Liturgy on the previous Sunday.

thanks to God with the words, "Let us give thanks to the Lord," the celebrant leads the entire congregation toward the completion of the Bloodless Sacrifice. The choir responds to this exhortation of thanksgiving with the response, "It is worthy and right." Indeed, it is worthy for all to be present, in the sacred precincts of that particular temple and for that holy purpose—the Divine Eucharist. Next the priest urges the congregation in the chanting of the Triumphal Hymn, "Singing, crying, shouting the Triumphal Hymn, and saying," to which the people respond, "Holy, Holy Lord of Hosts, heaven and earth are full of Your glory." Like the prosphoro itself, which is stamped with the inscription ΙΣ ΧΣ ΝΙ ΚΑ, the faithful now sing a victory hymn both glorifying our Lord's victory over the powers of darkness and death, and at the same time bringing to mind His second coming as victor. The Cherubic Hymn is a song of praise for yesterday, today, and tomorrow!

17

Following the prayer of the Anaphora, the priest incarnates the Mystical Supper—our Lord's saving Sacrifice—when He gave His pure Body and precious Blood to His disciples, "Take, eat, this is my Body, which is broken for you for the forgiveness of sins . . . Drink of this all of you, this is my Blood of the new covenant, shed for you and for many for the forgiveness of sins." The liturgical celebrant invokes the Holy Spirit and entreats God to transform the elements into the Body and Blood of our Lord.

The Divine Eucharist unites us with our All-pure Lady, the Most-holy Theotokos, "Especially for our most holy, most pure, and blessed Lady," together with the souls of every person who has drawn near to and been united with God, "Forefathers, Fathers, Patriarchs, Prophets, Apostles, Preachers, Evangelists, Martyrs, Confessors, Ascetics, and every righteous spirit made perfect in faith." The celebrant elevates the Lamb-Christ above the diskarion after the holy Gifts have become the Body and Blood of our Lord and Savior Jesus Christ, saying, "The Holy things for the Holy." This liturgical action symbolizes the Lord's elevation on the Cross, His Crucifixion, and His Resurrection—and those who are prepared to partake of this wondrous mystery are invited to draw near to Him.

After the priest says, "The Holy things for the Holy," the Lamb is "broken and distributed, broken yet not divided, ever eaten and yet never consumed" into four parts that are arranged on the diskarion in the form of a Cross, ΙΣ at the top, ΧΣ at the bottom, ΝΙ at

the left, and KA at the right. The portion of the Body
of Christ stamped with ΙΣ is placed into the Chalice
and united with the Blood of Christ. Next, hot water
is added to the Chalice. The mingling of the Body and
Blood signifies that Christ is One, while the addition
of the hot water signifies that Christ is living and is
Life itself, and also symbolizes the descent of the Holy
Spirit as tongues of fire upon the disciples at Pentecost. The clergy commune from the second portion of
the Lamb first, and then from the Chalice. The remaining portions of the Lamb are added to the Chalice pri-
or to distribution of Holy Communion to the faithful.

19

Standing before the congregation, the priest holds in
his hands the most sublime Mystery of the Church. He
invites those gathered for the synaxis to approach the
sacrificed and risen Christ with "the fear of God, with
faith and with love," and to receive the spotless Body
and precious Blood of our Lord. When we receive Holy
Communion we are united to God and to the plenitude
of holy souls throughout all of history who have been
joined to Christ through the holy Chalice.

After the faithful have received the Divine Eucharist, the priest places the remaining excised portions
from the prosphoro into the holy Chalice, including

the particles for the living and the reposed, while saying, "Wash away, Lord, the sins of those commemorated by Your precious Blood through the intercession of the Theotokos and all the saints." Following the Dismissal of the Divine Liturgy, the priest will consume the remaining contents of the holy Chalice during the recitation of the Prayers of Thanksgiving.

d. The Prosphoro Seal

20

Every prosphoro is embossed using a stamp prior to baking. In ancient times, stamps were made of clay; more recently, they have been made of wood and even plastic.

The Five Parts of the Prosphoro Seal are:

In the center of the seal there is a square with a four quadrant Cross and the inscription ΙΣ ΧΣ ΝΙ ΚΑ. This part of the stamped prosphoro is called the Lamb, which becomes the Body of Christ during the Divine Liturgy.[7] After stamping and baking, the inscription

---

7. The description of the Lord as Lamb can be traced to the Prophecy of Isaiah: "And because he was afflicted, he does not open his mouth; like a sheep is led to slaughter, and like a lamb is voiceless before the one who shears it, so he does not open his mouth" (Isaiah 53:7). This was confirmed by the Forerunner, Saint John the

on the prosphoro should be clear and undistorted. The excision of the Lamb from the prosphoro and its placement on the diskarion is accompanied by the words, "And His life was taken up from the earth," which recalls the Lord's prophecy concerning Himself: "And I, if I am lifted up from the earth, will draw all [people] to myself" (John 12:32).

To the right of the Lamb is the portion designated for the Most-holy Theotokos and is inscribed with the Greek letters Μ Θ, an abbreviation for Μήτηρ Θεοῦ (Mother of God). The Panagia is the Queen of Heaven, an honor that our Lord gave to His own mother, prophetically announced in the psalmic verse, "The queen is near at your right side, clothed in apparel interwoven with gold, adorned with embroidery" (Ps. 44:10). As the celebrant excises the portion for the Mother of God, he says, "In honor and memory of our most blessed and glorious Lady, the Theotokos and ever-virgin Mary, through whose intercessions, O Lord, accept this offering upon your heavenly table," and then placing it

21

Baptist, who indicated Jesus to his disciples, saying, "Behold, the Lamb of God who takes away the sin of the world!" (John 1:29).

on the diskarion he recites the verse referenced above, "The queen is near . . ."

To the left of the Lamb is a grouping of nine triangles of prosphora that represent the angelic and saintly orders who are mystically present at the celebration of every Divine Liturgy. These triangles are individually excised, beginning from the triangle on the top left of the first grouping and continuing on in three vertical columns from left to right: 1) holy Angels, Prophets, Apostles, 2) Martyrs, Hierarchs, Ascetics, 3) Unmercenary Healers, Joachim and Anna, the saint commemorated on that day, and finally the saint-author of the Divine Liturgy to be celebrated, either Saint John Chrysostom or Saint Basil the Great.

The inscribed portions above and below the Lamb are excised for the commemoration of the living and the reposed. The first excision is for the presiding hierarch of the parish, which the priest places directly below the Lamb. Then the priest begins his commemorations for the living, starting with the hierarch who ordained him (if he is living), and then whomever else he wishes to commemorate. After the celebrant commemorates the living, he then proceeds to remember those who have fallen asleep in the Lord, beginning with the hierarch who ordained him (if he is reposed), and then whomever else he wishes.

The design of the stamp will vary according to local custom. For example, in Romania it is common to see only the inscription ΙΣ ΧΣ ΝΙ ΚΑ on the central portion of the seal. In Russia, it is customary for the Lamb to be excised from a single small prosphoro. The common element in all local seal traditions is the central placement of the Lamb with the inscription ΙΣ ΧΣ ΝΙ ΚΑ.

e. Antidoron

As mentioned above, *antidoron* means "instead of the Gift," where the gift is the Divine Eucharist, the Body and Blood of the Lord Jesus Christ. Specifically, antidoron is blessed bread offered to those faithful who, for whatever reason, were unable to receive Holy Communion during the Divine Liturgy.[8]

Antidoron comes from the bread out of which the Lamb was excised; in other words, from the prosphoro that was sanctified and offered to God at the Service of Preparation. Its distribution is a means of "transmitting ineffable blessings to those who partake of it

23

---

8. Today, it is common practice for all those present to receive antidoron, whether or not a person has received Holy Communion.

with faith."[9] Because the Church, as our dear Mother, always extends her unique and wondrous care to her children, she offers this spiritual blessing to all of the faithful who have gathered for the celebration of the Divine Liturgy, and especially to her children who have not partaken of the Gift of all gifts, her Son and our Lord and Savior.

Antidoron does not take the place of the Divine Eucharist. The proper and regular participation in the Mystery of Holy Communion should be the heartfelt desire of all Orthodox Christians.

---

9. Saint Germanos, *Contemplation*, in *Patrologia Graeca* 98.452D.

The Preparation
of Prosphoro and Artoclasia Bread

CHAPTER TWO

a. Prosphoro

Prosphoro is prepared in a variety of ways, though these are more or less similar. In the modern period it has become common to find recipes for the preparation of prosphoro with commercially made yeast[1] rather than traditional fermented starter (also called "leaven") made in the home. The reason for this is obvious—traditional starter requires more time and planning, something that is often in short supply in the daily lives of modern-day Orthodox Christians. While commercial yeast might be helpful in short-

---

1. Commercially made yeast comes in three varieties: instant (very fast acting), active dry (fast acting), and "fresh."

ening the preparation time of prosphoro, the effects are often unpredictable and the results less than satisfactory. The most common problems caused by the use of commercial yeast concern difficulties during stamping and the disappearance or distortion of the seal during baking.

Compared to modern commercially made yeasts, traditional fermented starter is a tried and true method that produces more predictable and superior results. It produces the highest quality embossing, and the texture of the bread is much firmer and better suited to excision during the Service of Preparation. The use of traditional starter also encourages patience and vigilance, both ascetic virtues and spiritual blessings.

28

One venerable tradition is to prepare the starter using blessed basil from the Feast of the Exaltation of the Precious Cross on September 14. However, this is not required. Starter can be made at any time, with or without blessed basil. If for some reason a person is unable to prepare the starter she can ask another prosphoro baker to share some of their starter.

Preparing Traditional Starter

INGREDIENTS

A sprig of blessed basil from the Feast of the
Exaltation of the Cross (optional)[2]

60 gr high-protein bread unbleached flour[3]

60 gr pure, non-chlorinated water (room
temperature)

OTHER NEEDS

Glass or ceramic jar for storing the starter[4]

Flour sifter

Digital kitchen scale

Whisk

Tablespoon

---

2. If you plan to use blessed basil, please note that it must be fresh
and alive. Keep the basil in a vase with holy water until you are
ready to prepare the starter.

3. High-protein flour has at least 12% protein. The editor prefers
Bob's Red Mill Artisan Bread Flour, which has 12–14% protein. You
should plan to use the same flour for both the starter and the prosphoro you plan to bake.

4. King Arthur Baking Company sells a ceramic crock for storing
traditional fermented starter.

DIRECTIONS

Begin by carefully washing and thoroughly drying your hands. Using a whisk, mix the sifted flour and water until it resembles a thick paste. Ensure that the ingredients are well mixed and that no lumps of dry flour remain.

While chanting or reciting the apolytikion of the Precious Cross, place the basil in the shape of a Cross on top of the paste-like mixture:

Save O Lord Your people and bless Your inheritance, ∗ granting victory to the faithful over the enemies, ∗ and by Your Cross preserving Your commonwealth.

We may also say the Kontakion of the Cross:

You who were lifted on the Cross voluntarily, ∗ O Christ our God, bestow Your tender compassions ∗ upon Your new community to which You gave Your name. ∗ Cause our faithful emperors to be glad in Your power, ∗ granting them the victories against their adversaries. ∗ And for an ally, Lord, may they have You, ∗ peace as their armor, the trophy invincible.

Loosely cover the jar and set this mixture aside to begin the process of fermentation.

On the following day, remove the basil, add the same amount of flour and water to the mixture, whisk thoroughly, chant the apolytikion, replace the basil, and set aside for another twenty-four hours.

On the third day, discard about 60 gr of the starter, and repeat the process; however, today do not replace the basil. Instead, carefully allow the blessed basil to dry out and then burn it or place it outside on the ground in a secluded spot where it can naturally disintegrate and not be trampled underfoot.

By the third day, you should observe small bubbles in the starter and detect a mild acidic odor. You should notice that the mixture rises and falls after feedings of additional flour and water, indicating that the starter is alive.

Continue this process once a day: remove 60 gr of the active starter, then add 60 gr of flour and water, whisk thoroughly, and set aside.

This process can continue indefinitely for as long as you wish to keep your starter alive. All you need to do is to continue to feed and care for it. If you are unable to care for your starter due to travel or some other situation, simply seal the jar containing your starter and place it in the refrigerator.

By the end of the first week the starter should be ready for use. You can test some of your starter by placing a teaspoon of it in a small bowl of fresh water. If the starter floats, it is ready for use.

While it is not common, it is possible that, even after carefully following the above instructions, a starter can fail to grow or seem to spontaneously die. This can happen due to the intrusion of contaminants into the starter or from a failure to properly feed and care for it. In either case you will detect an unpleasant odor and a breakdown of the starter and the presence of a grayish tint in the mixture. If this happens, discard the starter and begin the process again.

It is a good idea to have at least two containers for storing your starter. This is because the use of one container can lead to problems with mold. Thus the authors advise that you transfer your starter to a clean jar every couple of weeks.

If you have excess starter due to daily feedings, simply remove a greater quantity of active starter, for example, 100 gr. However, always be mindful to feed with equal quantities of flour and water.

Preparing Your Work Area

Before making prosphoro, it is important to make sure your prep area is spotlessly clean. Kneading the dough requires a clean countertop or kneading bowl. If you plan to use an electric mixer, then please make sure it has been recently washed and is free of any food debris. Ideally, all of your tools and vessels should be set aside and reserved for prosphoro preparation and baking and not used for other purposes.

PREP AND BAKING NEEDS

A kneading bowl, either earthenware, wood, or stainless steel, or an electric mixing bowl[5]

A flour sifter to ensure no impurities spoil the prosphoro

High-sided round pans for baking[6]

Instant-read digital thermometer

33

5. There are strong opinions among some people about the use of electric mixers for prosphoro preparation. Kneading by hand is certainly a venerable method and carries with it an ascetic quality, but it does not thereby make a "better" prosphoro.

6. While high-sided pans are not required they are highly suggested. A high-sided pan with a 4-inch depth helps the prosphoro retain its shape during proofing and baking. The editor recommends the Fat Daddio brand, which is available from Amazon in diameters from 4 to 16 inches. See p. 105.

Initial Prep

Verify that you have all the necessary ingredients in the exact quantities needed to make the number of prosphora you intend to bake. The ingredients *must* be fresh—do not use anything past its stated expiration date! Also, do not mix flour types and brands. You should have enough flour of a single brand and type, and ideally the same flour type and brand that you used to prepare your starter. *Do not expect reliable results if you use different flours.*

PREPARING THE PAN

The pan must be prepared before kneading. Thoroughly clean one or more high-sided round pans. The size of the pan should be based on the size of the seal that will be used. Refer to the table on page 36 for help in choosing the correct size baking pan.

Rather than using nonstick pans with industrial coatings such as Teflon, it is recommended that the interior of the pan be coated with natural beeswax. This will provide a superior nonstick surface for prosphoro baking. The extra time needed for this step is well worth the effort.

Place a high-sided pan on the stove and turn the heat to medium-high. After the pan has been thoroughly warmed, put on a pair of oven mitts and use a few sheets of folded paper towel to clean the interior of the pan while paying close attention to the seams at the base of the sides of the pan. If there is debris from previous use, simply re-fold the paper towel and continue to wipe the pan until nothing remains and it is thoroughly heat-cleaned.

Once the pan has been heat-cleaned, add about 5 gr of pure beeswax (do not use any other kind of wax) to the pan and allow it to melt. Once the beeswax has completely melted, take a couple of sheets of folded paper towel and use them to thoroughly spread the beeswax on all sides of the pan, including the base and sides. Pay close attention to the seams of the base of the pan and make sure that they are also coated. Continue to use the paper towels until there is a shiny coating of beeswax throughout the pan. Ensure that there are no "puddles" of beeswax. After coating the pan, remove it from the heat and set it aside on a baking rack to cool. Repeat this procedure if you plan to bake more than a single prosphoro.

MEASURING THE INGREDIENTS

Place your kneading bowl or electric mixing bowl on a digital kitchen scale[7] and begin adding ingredients according to the amounts specified in the following table. Note the proportions, which can be easily adjusted for any size prosphoro that you wish to bake;[8] what follows are simply some options. If you intend to make two prosphora, double your quantities.

SEAL SIZE	PAN SIZE	FLOUR	WATER	STARTER	SALT
10.5-11 cm	6 in	400 gr	200 gr	20-30 gr	4 gr
16 cm	8 in	800 gr	400 gr	40-50 gr	8 gr
17 cm	10 in	1000 gr	500 gr	50-60 gr	10 gr

INITIAL MIXING AND REST PERIODS

Once all the ingredients have been added to the bowl, begin mixing with your hands for a few minutes—and remember, you are not kneading dough, but mixing ingredients. At this stage the mixture will look rough. Continue mixing until all the ingredients have

7. A digital kitchen scale is essential for repeatable results. Do not rely on measuring cups or spoons.

8. The proportions are intended to produce a 51% hydration dough. A dough of these proportions will be extremely easy to handle and will not stick to the prosphoro stamp.

been incorporated and they begin to form a "dough." At this stage the dough will be lumpy, but without any unincorporated dry bits of flour. If mixing by hand, this should take 5–10 minutes. If you are using an electric mixer, this stage should take 2.5–5 minutes depending on the power and efficiency of the mixer.[9] Once this stage has been reached (See images of dough at various stages of the kneading and rest periods on page 109), then place the mixture into an appropriately sized Ziploc bag, or other sealed container to autolyze for 30 minutes.

This important stage allows time for the flour to completely hydrate and for the gluten to begin bonding and developing. Following this procedure will reduce the overall kneading time in the next step. Do not skip this step!

KNEADING AND SECONDARY REST PERIODS

After the 30 minute autolysis stage has been completed, remove the dough from the Ziploc bag and

9. The editor has tested various electric mixing tools, including KitchenAid (4.7 liter) and Anksarum (7 liter) stand mixers, as well as kneading machines such as the Bear Dough Maker (5 liter), and cooking robots such as the Thermomix TM6 (2.2 liter). Of these tools, the editor prefers the Bear and the TM6.

place it in the kneading bowl or electric mixing bowl to begin the process of finishing the dough.

Begin kneading or electric-mixing in three periods. Follow the table below.

KNEADING METHOD	KNEADING TIME	REST PERIOD
By Hand	8-10 mins x 3	10 mins x 3
Electric (Bear Dough Maker)	3-5 mins x 3	10 mins x 3
Electric (Thermomix TM6)	2.5 mins x 3	10 mins x 3
Electric (KitchenAid 5qt or similar)	5 mins x 3	10 mins x 3

Each kneading or mixing period is followed by a 10 minute rest period. During the rest period, the mixing bowl should be covered by a clean damp kitchen towel to prevent the dough from drying. When using an electric mixing tool it is important not to over-mix, which can potentially damage the dough by overheating.

As you complete each mixing stage, the dough will become smoother and smoother. By the final kneading period, if the proper proportions and quantities were observed during the measuring stage, the dough will not stick to your fingers or hands. If, however, for some reason the dough is sticking to your hands then add a very small amount of flour (in 50 gr increments) and fully incorporate it into the dough. Repeat until you achieve a smooth consistency. On the other hand, if for some reason the dough has not achieved a consistent smooth form, you may add a very small amount of pure, non-chlorinated water in 20 gr increments and fully incorporate it into the dough until you achieve a smooth dough consistency.[10]

SHAPING AND STAMPING

After the third resting period, the dough is shaped and prepared for stamping.[11] What follows is an attempt to describe the shaping process, but please note that there are many ways to shape a prosphoro. Do what works for you. The end result should be a very smooth, ball-shaped loaf with a flat bottom.

39

There should be no need to flour your work area—your dough should not be sticky. To aid in this

10. If you add flour or water to the dough after the autolysis phase, then you will need to observe additional resting periods to allow for proper hydration of the dough to occur. The editor has noticed that this is never necessary when exact weighted quantities are used during the measuring.
11. If you are making two or more prosphora, weigh the dough and cut it into equal portions. Since you will be shaping one loaf at a time, place the additional portion(s) of dough in a sealed container to prevent it from drying out.

process, be sure to work on a smooth, nonporous surface.

In order to shape the dough, place it on your clean workspace and roll the dough to smooth it. Once you have a relatively smooth and roundish ball, pull the dough outward and up to create a teardrop shape. This will allow you to create an even smoother surface by stretching the dough. At the pointy end of the teardrop-shaped dough ball, squeeze and tighten the ends that you pulled to smooth the surface of the ball. Press your fingers into the pointy end to flatten it and make sure that there are no air pockets.[12] Now place the dough ball on the counter and gently roll it on the teardrop end and smooth it and gently press it down to *slightly* flatten it. Now take the dough into your hands and roll it on the counter. By repeating these steps you should be able to create a very smooth ball of dough with a slightly flattened bottom. Remember to be gentle, and do not over-flatten the dough. See the relevant photos on pages 111–115 for tips on the various stages of the shaping process.

---

12.   A rolling pin is useful at the beginning of the shaping process.

Once you have achieved the desired shape, carefully lift the dough from the workspace and place it into your prepared high-sided pan. Once the dough is positioned in the center of the pan, cover it with a damp kitchen towel and let it rest for 15 minutes. Do not skip this step. While resting, the dough will slightly spread out due to gravity. This is normal and of no concern.

Once 15 minutes have elapsed, remove the damp kitchen towel and gently "paint" a nearly imperceptible coating of flour on the top and sides of the dough. To do this, dip a dry pastry brush into the flour and knock it against the sides of the flour container to remove any excess. Then very gently paint the dough. It is better to return to the flour and add a little more of it than to over-flour the dough on the first pass. There should be no visible particles of flour on the dough.

It is now time to stamp the dough—to create a prosphoro! Make the Sign of the Cross while saying, "In the name of the Father, and the Son, and the Holy Spirit," three times over the dough with the stamp. Center the stamp over the dough by checking the stamp's location from all angles. You can ever-so-gently allow the stamp to rest on the top of the dough and make the necessary adjustments before stamping. Once you have done your best to center the stamp, firmly press down on the center of the stamp with the heel of your palm. Try to stamp the dough evenly, avoiding a tilted impression, since this will negatively affect the final result during the rise and baking of the prosphoro.

Carefully remove the seal by gently lifting straight up from the handle of the seal. The seal should cleanly release from the surface of the prosphoro with a firm level pull. You may need to rotate the pan a few times and gently pull up on the seal before it releases.

Do not panic if the seal does not at first seem to release from the surface of the dough. If this happens, very gently press the dough away from the seal toward the edge of the pan. Try to avoid deforming the dough. If this step is necessary, make very careful movements. After the dough has been pushed away from the seal in four opposite directions—as in 12, 3, 6, and 9 o'clock—try to lift the seal again. Repeat if necessary.

After removing the seal from the top surface of the prosphoro, the surface is pierced with a needle or toothpick. Take care not to damage the seal. Typically, a prosphoro is pierced on the corners of the central lamb and around the outer ridge, which is outside the impression. While some people make twelve equally spaced punctures on the outer ridge in honor of the twelve holy Apostles, others make thirty-three for the years of our Lord's life, while still others make fewer.

RISING

After piercing the surface of the prosphoro, set it aside to let it rise. If you plan to use a proofing box or oven with proof setting, set the temperature to 80°F. Alternatively, the prosphoro may be placed under a cake dome, though it should not be tightly sealed. To avoid this, simply place something under the edge of the cake dome to allow air to circulate. Rising takes approximately 6-10 hours. See pages 116-117 to better understand the amount of rise that you can expect to see.

43

Baking problems will result if the prosphoro is under- or over-risen; here, patience and vigilance are both necessary. Under-rising will cause the prosphoro to tear during baking. Over-rising can result in either the loss of the seal's impression, or an overly dense prosphoro if it is permitted to deflate. To avoid this, set a timer and keep watch from the 6th hour mark onward. When ready, the prosphoro should be about double its original height with the seal still fully visible. You will also notice that the center surface of the prosphoro, where the seal was impressed, should have risen to be slightly higher than the pierced outer ridge. Some people suggest using a press test on the dough to determine bake readiness. To do this, press a finger in the pierced outer ridge of the prosphoro causing a quarter-inch depression. Hold for a few seconds. Release and take note of how the dough responds. If the dough springs back immediately, the rise is incomplete. If the dough does not spring back at all, the rise is late. If the dough springs back slowly, the rise is complete.

44

Mastering the rise takes practice, and failures are inevitable. Keep a simple log that records the total rising time and any baking problems observed. If tearing occurs, increase the rise in the future. Likewise, if the seal disappears or if the prosphoro deflates, decrease the rise time.

A temperature adjustable box-type dehydrator may be helpful if poor definition or complete loss of the seal is a persistent problem. At the beginning of the rise, place the prosphoro in the dehydrator at 80 degrees for one to two hours. After no more than two hours, remove the prosphoro from the dehydrator and complete the rise in a proofing box or under a cake dome.

BAKING

Prosphoro should be baked in a preheated oven. When nearing the completion of the rise, set the oven to 350–365°F or 175–185°C. Since every oven has its own personality and characteristics, the baking process must be adjusted to fit the individual oven. Baking times are also dependent upon the size of the prosphoro. An 800 gr prosphoro will bake in about 50 minutes at 350–365°F. A small 300 gr loaf will bake in about 40 minutes, whereas a larger 1000 gr loaf will requires a baking time of about 60 minutes. When learning, it is advisable to check the baking prosphoro in 15 minute increments, so that you can familiarize yourself with the process.

After the rise is complete and the oven has reached the desired temperature, place the pan containing the prosphoro in the center of the oven cavity. Avoid placing the pan near the edges of the cooking chamber. Doing so will result in hot-spots on the surface of the prosphoro. After baking for 15 minutes, check the prosphoro to verify that no large bubble or "oven spring" has occurred. If a bubble is noticed, take a toothpick and pierce it. Then carefully press down on that area with an oven mitt. After about 20–30 minutes, for an 800 gr or greater prosphoro, cover the top of the pan with a piece of aluminum foil to prevent the surface from becoming too brown. A smaller prosphoro, which requires a shorter baking time, should be covered earlier in the baking process.

Recognizing when the prosphoro is properly finished comes with experience. When fully baked, the top surface of the prosphoro should have a light golden color and a hollow, drum-like sound when tapped from the bottom after it has been removed from the pan.

TEMPERATURE

To verify doneness, check the internal temperature of the prosphoro. For loaves of 800 gr or more, the temperature of the prosphoro may be checked after 45 minutes by using an instant-read digital thermometer with probe. The probe must be inserted from the bottom to the center of the loaf. This requires the prosphoro to be briefly removed from the oven, carefully removed from the pan, and inverted. If the probe reads 190°F or more, baking is complete. If the prosphoro requires additional time, put it back in the pan, cover it with foil, and place it in the center of the cooking chamber for another 5–10 minutes.

OVENS

When using a non-conventional oven—such as a convection or a steam oven—cooking times must be tried and adjusted on a case by case basis. For example, convection cooking uses fans to circulate air within the cooking chamber and therefore will shorten the bake time. Thus proceed with caution when using convection and begin by working at temperatures up to 25°F lower than those used with a conventional oven.

47

COOLING AND DELIVERY

After the prosphoro has finished baking, remove it from the pan, enclose it in a clean, unused, and unscented kitchen towel[13] and place it on a cooling rack. It can take roughly 6 hours for the prosphoro to fully

---

13. Towels used in cooling and transporting prosphoro should have been washed in an odorless detergent and dried without scented dryer sheets.

cool, and all during this time the loaf should remain in the towel. Once the prosphoro has completely cooled, it can be placed in a Ziploc bag or covered with cling wrap.

Some people use embroidered fabric carriers for transporting prosphoro to church, and while this is a respectable practice, it is not necessary. Delivery time, however, is essential. Consult the priest to find out when he needs the prosphoro. Delivering the prospho-ro at Vespers the evening before the Divine Liturgy is advisable to avoid inconveniencing the priest. Do not assume anything—ask what is preferable and make plans accordingly.

STEAM GLAZING (OPTIONAL STEP)

Steam glazing produces a sheen on the top surface of the prosphoro. The purpose of this treatment is wholly aesthetic,[14] and therefore completely option-al. In order to successfully steam glaze a prosphoro, it must be hot out of the oven. Do not plan to offer a steam glazed prosphoro without the blessing of the priest. If the priest is unfamiliar with the technique,

---

14. Steam glazing does not effect the internal consistency of the loaf.

he should be reassured that the only element used in this process is water.

Applying the steam glaze, while not difficult, must be done with care to avoid personal injury and other fiascoes.

> A proper size saucepan is required for steam glazing. Ensure that the saucepan is at least 1.5–2 inches smaller in diameter than the prosphoro. Using a pan of the same, or larger, diameter risks the accidental loss of the loaf into the boiling water.

While the prosphoro is baking, fill a saucepan with 1–2 inches of water and place it on the stove top. After determining that the prosphoro is fully cooked, as described above, remove it from the oven and its baking pan and wrap the loaf in a clean kitchen towel. Turn the temperature of the burner with the water-filled saucepan to high. Be sure to have both hands fully covered in good quality oven mitts to avoid burns.[15]

After the water comes to a boil, remove the prosphoro from the towel and lightly brush the entire top

49

---

15. Do not use pot holders for this process! Water-resistant silicon mitts are preferred, because they will not allow the steam to penetrate the mitts and cause burns to the skin.

surface of the hot prosphoro with boiling water using a good quality pastry brush. Now take the loaf, invert it, and hold it 1 inch above the steaming water for about 30 seconds. Repeat this process three times. While it may be tempting to allow the prosphoro to sit directly on the rim of the saucepan, this is not recommended for two reasons: 1) the loaf may slip into the water, and 2) the boiling water may splash the loaf if the saucepan is not very deep.

50

The noticeable sheen on the top surface of the prosphoro will gradually intensify after each repetition. However, take care not to over-steam the loaf, which will cause bubbles to appear on its surface. When you have completed the process three times, set the loaf aside to cool. Wait about 45 minutes before covering the steam-glazed prosphoro with a clean kitchen towel. The glazed surface will remain glossy, even after the prosphoro has completely cooled.

THE COMMEMORATION LIST FOR PROSPHORO

Your commemoration list should be thoughtfully prepared at home, not as an afterthought while standing in the narthex of the church. The commemoration list should include the first baptismal name of each living and reposed Orthodox Christian that you would like the priest to commemorate at the Table of Preparation[16] on a columnar list. Catechumens may be included. Do not use nicknames,[17] last names, or shorthand such as "The Smith Family." Write out the names of each family member, including the children if you know their names. Clergy should be named with their appropriate ecclesiastical office.[18] Be careful to write names legibly, in an easy-to-read print, rather than cursive. You should not write names in a foreign language, unless you are certain that the priest is able to read that language.

51

b. Artoclasia Bread

Preparing bread for the service of the Blessing of the Loaves (Artoclasia) is similar to preparing prosphoro. The traditional recipe presented here is suitable for

---

16. The practice of the Orthodox Church is to limit our liturgical commemorations to Orthodox Christians—those who are united to Christ's Holy Body, the Church. Of course we may, and should, pray for non-Orthodox Christians in our personal prayers.

17. For example, "Dimitrios" rather than "Jimmy Papadopoulos," and "Stavroula" rather than "Voula Petrakis."

18. For example, "John the Hierarch," "George the Priest," "Peter the Hieromonk," "Elizabeth the Nun" (or "Monastic"), and so on.

all days and feasts—in other words, it does not include any non-Lenten ingredients. This recipe[19] uses the same natural leaven as the prosphoro recipe above. The basic recipe will yield five 6-inch round loaves.[20]

BASIC RECIPE

2000 gr high-protein flour[21]

200 gr natural leaven

67 gr sugar

205 gr dark brown sugar

85 gr Earth Balance® at room temperature[22]

10 gr ground cinnamon

500 gr orange juice (no pulp)[23]

500 gr apple juice (no pulp)

20 gr salt

---

19. It is important to plan ahead and make sure that there is enough natural leaven prepared for the recipe. It is simple to build up the amount of leaven by adding additional flour and water in equal parts to your leaven jar a day or two before you plan to prepare the loaves.

20. To make larger loaves, double the recipe.

21. See footnote 3 in this chapter.

22. Earth Balance comes in different varieties. The variety suggested is *Original Buttery Spread*.

23. If a sweeter loaf is desired, use 1000 gr of apple juice rather than orange juice.

5 tbs sesame seeds
5 6x4 in high-sided pans
5 10x10 in sheets of aluminum foil
350°F preheated oven
Instant-read digital thermometer

MEASURING THE INGREDIENTS FOR ARTOCLASIA

Place your kneading bowl or electric mixing bowl on a digital kitchen scale[24] and begin adding ingredients according to the amounts specified in the recipe on the previous page. If the Earth Balance has not been brought to room temperature, simply place the hard spread in a microwave-safe bowl in a microwave oven for 10–20 seconds to soften and partially melt it.

53

MIXING AND REST PERIODS FOR ARTOCLASIA

Once all the ingredients have been added to the bowl, begin mixing with your hands for a few minutes. You will notice that the artoclasia mixture will be slightly more sticky than the prosphoro mixture; however, when all stages have been completed, it should not stick to your hands if you have measured the ingredients correctly.

---

24. See footnote 7 in this chapter.

Observe the same mixing times and rest periods as specified for preparing prosphoro by following the instructions on page 36 where it says, "Continue mixing until all the ingredients have been incorporated . . ." Remember to prepare the pans using beeswax as described above on page 35.

During the last 10-minute rest/mix period, boil 4 cups of water in a small saucepan. When the water comes to a boil, remove the saucepan from the heat and add the sesame seeds to the water. Set a timer for 2 minutes. After 2 minutes, pour the water and sesame seeds through a fine strainer to collect the seeds. Set the wet sesame seeds aside.

After the completion of the third 10-minute rest/mix period, divide the dough into five equal portions (about 715 gr each). Form the loaves as described in the prosphoro instructions on pages 39–40. Once formed, place each portion of dough into one of the beeswax-prepared 6x4 in high-sided pans. Rather than resting the dough to stamp it, simply press it into the pan and distribute it evenly, making sure the surface is flat and level, with no high points or valleys. Now place a tablespoon of the wet sesame seeds on each flattened portion of dough and spread them evenly on the surface. Press the sesame seeds onto the flat surface of each round loaf. Set the loaves aside in a proofing box or an oven with its lights turned on and let the dough rise for 8–10 hours, or until the dough has doubled in size.

BAKING ARTOCLASIA

Place the five pans in a preheated oven and set the timer for 30 minutes. After the timer goes off, loosely cover the loaves with the prepared cut aluminum sheets to prevent the tops of the loaves from over-browning. Set the timer for 10 minutes. After the timer has sounded, remove the foil coverings and set them aside; do not discard them, as you will be using them again. Now, carefully remove the five loaves from their pans and place them directly on the oven rack. This will prevent the bottom and sides of the loaves from burning.[25] Recover the loaves with the cut aluminum sheets and set the timer for another 15 minutes. When the timer sounds, remove a single loaf from the oven, and while wearing an oven mitt, invert the loaf and check the temperature by inserting the probe of an instant-read digital thermometer through the bot-

---

25. To further deflect heat, you may place a few empty cookie sheets on the bottom rack of the oven.

tom to the approximate center of the loaf. If the test loaf has reached 190°F, remove the other loaves from the oven and place them on a cooling rack. If the test loaf has not reached 190°F, carefully place it back in its pan and put it back in the oven and set the timer for 5 minutes and retest the temperature when the timer sounds. Repeat if necessary to reach 190°F.

COOLING AND DELIVERY OF ARTOCLASIA

After the artoclasia loaves have finished baking, remove them from the oven, enclose them in clean, unused, and unscented kitchen towels[26] and place them on a cooling rack. If you have baked the loaves the day before they will be used, then you may safely keep them wrapped in towels. This will allow the loaves to retain a crunchy crust. Alternatively, after the loaves have cooled, you may place them in Ziploc bags or cover them with cling wrap, which will cause the crusts to soften.

In addition to the bread offering, wheat berries, ecclesiastical wine,[27] olive oil, and five beeswax tapers

---

26. Towels used in cooling and transporting artoclasia should have been washed in an odorless detergent and dried without scented dryer sheets.

27. Do not offer ordinary table wine, since it is unsuitable for use in the celebration of the Divine Liturgy. Speak with your priest

must also be obtained for the Service of Artoclasia. It is the responsibility of the individual who makes the offering to provide everything necessary for the service.

Some people coat the top of their artoclasia loaves with honey or powdered sugar. Do not do this without consulting your priest. Honey is sticky and powdered sugar is messy—they can dirty vestments, soil table coverings, and make the loaves awkward for the priest to handle during the service.

The Service of Artoclasia is part of the Service of Great Vespers.[28] Therefore, the loaves and other necessary elements must be delivered *well before* Great Vespers begins. Their decorous arrangement on a sacramental table takes time and care. Be sure to allow enough time to prepare the table. Do not disrupt the celebration of Great Vespers by arriving at the church late.

At the church, carefully arrange all of the items on the sacramental table in an attractive manner. If other individuals have also made artoclasia and have

well in advance to find out where ecclesiastical wine is available for purchase. If you cannot purchase the wine locally, ask if you can purchase it from the church.

28.   It is possible that your priest may celebrate the Service of Artoclasia at the conclusion of the Divine Liturgy.

already placed them on the sacramental table, ask for assistance from the priest, deacon, or caretaker, before moving anything.

THE COMMEMORATION LIST FOR ARTOCLASIA

Your commemoration list should be thoughtfully prepared at home, not as an afterthought while standing in the narthex of the church or in front of the sacramental table. The commemoration list should include the first baptismal name of each living[29] Orthodox Christian that you would like the priest to commemorate during the service.[30] Catechumens may be included, for example "John the Catechumen." Do not write nicknames,[31] last names, or use shorthand for familes, such as "The Smith Family." For the latter, write out the names of each family member, including the children if you know their names. Clergy should be named with their appropriate ecclesiastical office.[32] Be careful to write names legibly, in an easy-to-read print, rather than cursive. You should not write names

---

29. We do not commemorate reposed Orthodox Christians at the Service of Artoclasia.

30. See footnote 16 in this chapter.

31. See footnote 17 in this chapter.

32. See footnote 18 in this chapter.

in a foreign language, unless you are certain that the priest is able to read that language.

LORD JESUS CHRIST OUR GOD, who blessed the five loaves in the desert, and from them fed five thousand, bless these loaves also, this wheat, wine, and oil, and multiply them in this city (or land) and in all your world, and sanctify your faithful servants who partake of them.

Prayer of Blessing for the Service of Artoclasia

59

A sacramental table arranged for the Service of Artoclasia.

*Stories from the Lives of Saints
and Holy Elders*

CHAPTER THREE

From the Gerontikon

Saint Arsenios the Great once told the following story:

A certain uneducated ascetic, though he had made great strides in the practice of Christian living, fell into error on account of his simplicity. He would say, "The bread that we receive in Holy Communion is not the actual Body of Christ but is merely symbolic."

Two elders heard about this monk and his opinion. Since they knew his way of life, and that he was indeed a great ascetic, they thought that his mistaken view was due to his innocence and naivete. Therefore, they went to him and said, "Let us pray to God this week about this mystery [sacrament] of our faith, and we are confident that God will reveal the truth of the matter." The elder joyfully received this suggestion, and so prayed to God, saying, "Lord, you know that I am not a faithless person or motivated by evil intentions. Therefore, Lord Jesus Christ my God, show me the truth so that I am not foolishly led astray in ignorance." The other elders returned to their cells and entreated God in prayer . . . And God heard them all.

On the following Sunday, they went to church. The three sat together on cushions, with the unlettered elder sitting in the center. As the bread was placed on the Holy Table, the eyes of those three monks—and only those three—were opened, and the bread appeared to be a small child—the Christ Child! When the priest extended his hand to divide the bread into smaller portions, an angel of the Lord descended from the heavens holding a knife in his hand, sacrificed the Child, and poured His Blood into the Chalice.

When they approached to receive the Holy Mysteries, the simple elder alone received a portion of bloody meat. Seeing this frightful sight, he cried out, "Lord my God, I believe that the bread is Your Body and the Chalice contains Your Blood!" Immediately the meat in his hand took on the appearance of bread, as it was usually seen in the sacrament. Then the elder communed, thanking God. [Note that according to the ancient practice of the Church, the Body and Blood were received by the faithful separately. Today, this practice is preserved in the Divine Liturgy of Saint Iakovos the Brother of God. During that form of the liturgy, the faithful receive the Body of Christ in their hands, saying, "Amen," and then put the sacrament into their own mouth. After this they receive the Blood of Christ from the Chalice.]

The two other elders told the uneducated elder, "God knows that our human constitution cannot bear to consume human flesh. Therefore, He transforms bread into His Body and wine into His Blood, which the faithful can then receive with reverence." Those two elders thanked God, because He allowed their simple brother to retain the wages of his ascetic struggles. After this they joyfully returned to their cells.

The Venerable Theodosios the Koinoviarch

It was a feast day, but not just any feast day. It was the first and greatest of all the feasts, Holy Pascha. As the sacred evening of Great Saturday drew near, the brotherhood of Theodosios the Great found itself lacking in essential foodstuffs, including bread and oil. There were twelve brothers in all, and they were in great distress. They were grief-stricken, not merely because they lacked essential supplies for their own nourishment, but because they had no prosphoro. Without prosphoro, they would be unable to celebrate the Paschal Divine Liturgy, and thus receive Holy Communion. They assembled before their teacher and began to tell him of their concerns.

He said to them, "Simply prepare the Holy Table. Give no thought to anything else. The One who fed thousands of Israelites in the desert [Ex. 16:35], and who later satisfied the hunger of a great multitude [Matt. 14:19-21], will also look after us! Do you think He is less capable today, or unwilling to give generously of His benefactions?" This is how he spoke to his disciples concerning their worries.

Now we will tell you how his words were promptly realized, and how the brothers' hopes were fulfilled. In fact, it was like what occurred in ancient times when a ram appeared in the sabek bush for Abraham to sacrifice. The very same thing happened in this situation for that blessed elder.

After the sun had set, a person arrived with two mules carrying loads of various foodstuffs suitable for ascetics. Also present in those provisions was prosphoro for the Holy Table! The brethren were overjoyed for all that had happened. The supplies that this man brought to the brotherhood lasted until Pentecost.

The Venerable Theodore Sykeotes

One day, the Venerable Theodore Sykeotes (sixth-seventh centuries) was celebrating the divine services in Saint Antiochos the Martyr Church on the feast day of the Saint. When he elevated the diskarion with the Lamb (the excised portion of the prosphoro that was to be consecrated as the Body of Christ), he saw the Holy Bread unexpectedly elevate. It rose above the diskarion and settled back on the surface while making a joyful sound. The faithful witnessed the miracle in shock. Theodore glorified God for His divine favor in granting him to see this wonder.

There is another miracle involving the same Saint, which has been passed down through the generations. On this occasion, Saint Theodore was celebrating the Divine Liturgy with a dried-out prosphoro. In the congregation was a certain pious man, a patrician by the name of Photios. This man saw steam rising from the prosphoro, as if it had just been baked. A little later, when Photios received Holy Communion, he found that the bread was very dry. When he told the Saint what he had seen, Saint Theodore explained that this miracle had been visible only to him.

Saint Ahmet

Saint Ahmet the Neomartyr lived in Constantinople in the seventeenth century. He was an Ottoman and a Muslim. At one point he employed two extraordinarily pious Russian women. Whenever the older of the two women went to Divine Liturgy, she would return home with some holy water and antidoron for her younger sister. Each time this happened, Ahmet perceived an intense and uniquely pleasing scent coming from the woman's mouth. After much persistence, Ahmet extracted the secret from her. The younger sister explained that the pleasing scent occurred whenever she would consume the blessed antidoron that her older sister would bring to her. After hearing this, Ahmet wanted to see how Orthodox Christians worshiped. He disguised himself and went to the Patriarchal Church to attend a Divine Liturgy. While at the church, he was

granted God's grace to witness a second miracle: as the Patriarch exited the Beautiful Gate to bless the people, some unseen force elevated him off the ground while his body was enveloped in light. That light then spread out and fell upon all the members of the congregation except Ahmet himself! Amazed at what he had seen, Ahmet asked to be baptized. On May 3, 1682, he publicly confessed his faith in Christ and received the Martyr's crown.

Saint Nicholas Planas

Saint Nicholas Planas (reposed in 1932) celebrated the Divine Liturgy on every permissible day for about fifty years. Typically the faithful would bring him prosphora for the divine service. However, if no one brought him a prosphoro, he would buy one from a local bakery.

One day, when no one had brought him a prosphoro, the Saint became agitated. He sent someone to purchase a prosphoro from a local bakery; however, the bakery was sold out and indeed there were no prosphora to be found anywhere in the town.

Embarrassed, the Saint informed the congregation of the situation.

Saint Nicholas then turned back toward the Holy Table, and then immediately turned around again, now holding a fresh prosphoro! "My children, look!" the Saint said. "What an amazing divine sign!"

Saint Nicholas had found a prosphoro on the Holy Table . . .

Venerable Saint Iakovos Tsalikis

In August 1963, seventy-five craftsmen and workers from the village of Livantes arrived at the Sacred Monastery of the Venerable Ascetic David. These workmen, along with fifteen other workers who were already at the monastery, were going to build a cistern as a donation to the monks. Saint Iakovos oversaw the work, as well as the hospitality for the laborers. He had no money and each day the monastery's meager provisions were further emptied.

Eventually the day came when the monastery's resources were nearly exhausted. There were only about seven pounds of orzo (rice-shaped pasta) and one half of a prosphoro that would need to feed nearly one hundred men! Elder Efthimios offered another half of a loaf of bread. Saint Iakovos placed the orzo in a pot, together with the prosphoro and bread and went to the church. Standing before the icon of the Venerable David, the Saint entreated him to feed the workmen himself! Later, Saint Iakovos went to the kitchen and cooked the orzo with the little oil remaining. The whole company of laborers ate and there were leftovers. Saint Iakovos would later say, "Brethren, this miracle was a repeat of the feeding of the five thousand!"

Prosphora, Seals, and Bread
from Ancient to Modern

CHAPTER FOUR

T hough we don't often consider it, the preparation of prosphoro has a long-storied history. We will begin our examination of that history with pre-Christian cultures, and then proceed to ancient Roman Judea, the place of our Lord's incarnate ministry. From there, we will traverse the millennia until we reach the modern period. This journey will help us better appreciate the countless people who have prepared the bread of oblation as an offering of thanksgiving and supplication to God in honor of His many benefactions.

Wheat, Bread, and Wine in the Mediterranean

Bread has been the principal element in the diet of people living in the areas around the Mediterranean since prehistoric times. Archaeological evidence from Egypt, Mesopotamia, and Asia Minor help tell the story of bread, including the wheat used in its preparation, the shapes (round or oblong) of the loaves, and the method of baking (on coals or in an oven). Since ancient times, wheat flour was thought to be the most suitable type of flour for baking bread. For that reason, wheat bread—known even from the age of Homer— was a luxury and soon became associated with honorary or cultic offerings. Researchers have identified the ritual use of bread in cultural artifacts as early as the Minoan period. According to the Athenian lawmaker Solon (fifth century B.C.), only wheat bread shaped in rounds was appropriate for festal celebrations. Another example from the ancient Mediterranean comes from the Old Testament story of Ruth, in which Ruth partakes in the gathering of grain for the preparation of "presence bread" (Ruth 2). These loaves of bread were placed on a designated table in the ancient Temple in Jerusalem as an offering to God (Ex. 25:30). Compared to its prevalence in the Mediterranean, wheat was a little known grain in most of Africa, the Far East, and Oceania until the arrival of European colonizers.

Based on pre-Christian artifacts, we know that bread was often stamped. The ancient stamps that have been discovered (such as in pre-Christian Hellenistic Egypt, or later Pompeii circa the first century A.D.) indicate a usage beyond the cultic. These nonreligious stamps had practical purposes, such as notches to aid in baking and cutting, and symbols to indicate weight and origin. Some of these pre-Christian customs are still used today. There is both textual and artifactual evidence to show that religious stamps contain symbols or words of invocation. These stamps were made of clay, wood, metal, or stone.

A nonreligious relationship between bread and wine can also be found in antiquity. The Greek word Ἀκρατίζομαι [akratizome] means "to eat breakfast," in other words, a morning meal to give one energy for the day by eating ἀκράτισμα [akratisma], which is bread dipped in undiluted wine.[1] Eating akratisma for breakfast was a practice that persisted in the Byzantine and

73

---

1. See *Wealth*, by Aristophanes, line 295.

post-Byzantine periods and continued into the early modern period in parts of rural Greece, until its more recent replacement with coffee and tea. Related is the Greek phrase, λαβέ βουκάκρατον, which means, "take a piece of bread soaked in undiluted wine," and is found in the text of Abba Dorotheos concerning Abba Dositheos. From late antiquity into the early Christian period, this phrase meant, "Put something in your mouth to stop you from speaking—shut up!" We would be remiss not to mention Melchizedek from the Old Testament. This king-priest, a prototype of Christ the High Priest, welcomed Abraham (Gen. 14:18) with an offering of bread and wine in place of the customary animal sacrifice.

Bread and the Bread of Life

Christianity was born within this cultural milieu of the southeastern Mediterranean. The Lord used familiar cultural elements while guiding us on a "new way." It was within these preexisting pathways of culture that our Savior transformed something familiar into something new and wonderful.

Bread holds a place of great significance within the New Testament—the miracles of the Lord (Matt. 14:15-

21 and 15:32-38; Mark 6:34-43 and 8:1-9; Luke 9:12-17; John 6:5-13), His teachings (John 6:32-35 and 6:48-51), and the Lord's Prayer (Matt. 6:9-13) are all examples of this. Even the location of our Lord's birth—Bethlehem—means the "House of Bread." At the Mystical Supper, shortly before our Savior's arrest and sufferings, He shared bread and wine with His disciples, sanctifying them as His Body and Blood respectively (Matt. 26:26-30, Mark 14:17-25, Luke 22:14-23, John 13:18-30).

"Do this in memory of Me," said our Lord. According to His commandment, bread and wine received the foremost place in Christian worship—the Divine Eucharist. The earliest preserved references to the Sacrament occur in Acts of the Apostles (20:5-12) and Saint Paul's First Letter to the Corinthians (10:16-17), two works that date from the middle of the first century. From the founding of the Church until about the tenth century, the celebration of the Divine Liturgy developed into its present form. During that time, the Liturgy was gradually enriched with scriptural and theological content, while remaining faithful to what had been received from the Lord Himself and transmitted by Him to the holy Apostles: the reception of

75

Holy Communion—the precious Body and Blood of the Lord.

It appears that ordinary leavened bread was used in the early Church for the celebration of the Divine Liturgy. The Lord would have used this sort of bread at the Mystical Supper, which occurred on the eve of the Jewish Passover (the Feast of Unleavened Bread). The Lord Himself taught that "The Kingdom of Heaven is like the yeast that a woman took and mixed in with three measures of flour, until it was all leavened" (Matt. 13:33).[2]

16

We do not know exactly when Christians stopped using common leavened bread for the Divine Liturgy. However, this practice seems to have changed by the fourth century, since the *Life of Saint Pachomios the Great* mentions that monks must prepare prosphoro in silence. Prior to this, Christian symbols were inscribed on the top surface of common bread, which made it suitable for eucharistic purposes.

2. The use of unleavened bread for Holy Communion became commonplace in the West beginning in the ninth century. The adoption of this practice was one of the contributing factors that led to the eventual falling away of the western Church in the eleventh century.

Bread and Blessing

Apart from eucharistic bread, early Christian texts reveal that other breadstuffs were shared by the faithful on certain occasions such as a blessing. These texts tell of breads that were blessed by a bishop or priest to be made suitable for feast days of saints, sites of Christian pilgrimage, makaria meals or memorials, and as a blessing for the sick. A seventh-century work by Leontios, bishop of Neapolis of Cyprus, mentions that bread was shared among the faithful at Agape meals. Likewise, bread was exchanged between bishops, priests, and communities as an act of brotherly love. While early Christian texts speak of these breads of "blessing," they are brief and without substantial detail, and presume that the reader would be familiar with these practices. Some of these practices may have been carried over by the faithful from their pre-Christian roots, or were early Christian customs that were part of the developing Church, which at that time was still being severely persecuted. Thus, the expression "blessing" in these ancient texts, up until the fifth century, if not later, are nonspecific and could refer to a variety of practices. These early traditions might be comparable

to customs practiced today, such as the offering of artoclasia on significant feast days, the pious tradition of
baking and offering fanouropita in answer to prayers,
the preparation of Lazarakia on Lazarus Saturday, the
sharing of tsoureki on Holy Pascha, or the cutting of
vasilopita on New Year's Day. Nevertheless, the principal breadstuff for Christians, from the earliest days of
the Church until today, is the bread that was prepared,
offered, and used for the Mystery of Holy Communion
in the Divine Liturgy.

Bread Seals in Ancient Times

As mentioned above, eucharistic bread in the early Church was inscribed or stamped for symbolic and
practical purposes, but without a fixed pattern. Written records up to the ninth century provide little in-
formation on the form of ancient prosphoro seals;
however, archaeological evidence points to the possible forms of seals from that period. Due to widespread
turmoil in the Christian world until the third century,
whether from persecution or struggles against hereti-
cal movements, it appears that prosphoro seal-making
had not yet become a regular practice among the faithful. After the third century, there is archaeological ev-

idence from Egypt, the Middle East, Greece, and Italy of bread stamps with Christian symbols such as Crosses, birds (peacocks and doves), and fish. Most likely, stamps with these symbols were used in the blessings described above and by Christians for non-liturgical purposes. It is assumed that symbolic forms such as deer, grapes, fish, birds, stars, and palm branches arranged either in a triangular pattern for the Holy Trinity or in sets of four,[3] and combined with a Cross, characterized prosphoro seals of the fifth through the seventh centuries.

The name Christ has been, from the very beginning of Christian history, understood to possess unique power. The recitation of the name Christ as a weapon against demonic influence is mentioned in the New Testament.[4] The first two letters of "Christ" in Greek—the letters χ and ρ—were used to create a "Christogram," which was an iconic representation of the incarnate Lord for early Christians. The abbrevi-

---

3. The sets of four symbolically represented the phrase Χριστὸς Χριστιανοῖς Χαρίζει Χάριν ("Christ Graces Christians with Joy"), which itself repeats four times the letter X as the first letter of each term.

4. See Luke 10:17 and Acts 4:12.

ated use of the Lord's name by Saint Constantine the Great as a kind of insignia placed on military shields after his vision in 312 A.D.[5] certainly influenced such usage. This took a final form in Greek-speaking Orthodox Churches as ΙΣ ΧΣ ΝΙ ΚΑ (Jesus Christ Conquers), which is formed with the first and last letters of the two names "Jesus" and "Christ," ΙΣ ΧΣ,[6] combined with a portion of the message that Saint Constantine saw in his vision, ΝΙ ΚΑ.

We know that from at least the eighth century onward the portion of the prosphoro that is excised to become the Body of Christ has been called the "Lamb."[7] This Lamb portion was then sealed with the symbol of a Cross, which divided it into four quadrants with the

---

5. According to tradition, before his victory in the Battle of Milvian Bridge in 312, Saint Constantine the Great saw a chi-rho (χρ) in the sky along with the inscription "'Εν τούτῳ Νίκα" (In this, Victory).

6. In Greek, "Jesus" is spelled ΙΗΣΟΥΣ, and "Christ" is spelled ΧΡΙΣΤΟΣ. Hence the first and last letters of each word are ΙΣ ΧΣ.

7. See Saint Germanus of Constantinople, *On the Divine Liturgy: Translation*, ed. John Behr, trans. Paul Meyendorff, vol. 8, Popular Patristics Series (Crestwood, NY: Saint Vladimir's Seminary Press, 1984), 71: "The piece which is cut out with the lance signifies that 'Like a sheep he is led to the slaughter, and like a lamb that before its shearers is dumb.' "

The earliest known Eucharistic bread stamp (fourth century), found at Eisenberg, Central Germany.

SEAL 1

Greek letters IC | XC | NI | KA. This design was already in limited use by the sixth century and became widespread by the ninth. (See Seal 1)

A small group of pre-seventh century eucharistic seals that originate from Jerusalem, Sinai, and Greece are suggestive of the early Christian practice of receiving the Body and Blood of Christ separately, such as happens in the Divine Liturgy of Saint Iakovos the Brother of God. The surface of these seals

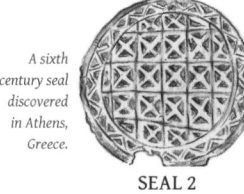

A sixth century seal discovered in Athens, Greece.

SEAL 2

are divided into many small squares with each containing an X. (See Seal 2) The prosphoro would have been subdivided along the lines of these small squares, and the communicant would have received one square of the Body of the Lord in his hand.

The Seal Today

The type of prosphoro seal used in Greece today was introduced during the post-Byzantine period. (See Seal 3) The elements of the design of this type of seal are IC XC NI KA / ΙΣ ΧΣ ΝΙ ΚΑ arranged around a Cross—the very same pattern that we previously men-

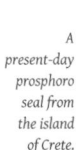

A present-day prosphoro seal from the island of Crete.

SEAL 3

tioned. This pattern is repeated three times on the surface of the seal, thus forming the vertical axis of a Cross. The horizontal axis is formed by symbolic elements for the angels, saints, and the Mother of God. The portion for the Mother of God is comprised of the abbreviation for Mother of God (Μήτηρ Θεοῦ), Μ Θ, which is typically flanked by a spear and a reed with a sponge, both symbols of the Lord's Passion. Theophanes the

82

Confessor, Bishop of Nicaea, explains the correlation between the Mother of God and the Passion, "For where else should Christ, that new victim, be forever present if not in her from

A present-day prosphoro seal from Saint Katherin Monastery, Sinai.

whom He was born . . . since there could be no place holier than her?"[8] The portion for the angels and saints is comprised of nine triangles in three rows of three, one for the angels and eight for the saints. The four gaps created by the cruciform design on the circular seal are typically filled with various decorations, such

8. Theophanes, Bishop of Nicaea, *Λόγος εἰς τὴν Παναγίαν Θεοτόκον* [*The Eulogy of the Holy Theotokos*], ed. M. Jugie (Rome: Facultas Theologica Pontificii Athenaei Seminarii Romani, 1935), 146.

A present-day prosphoro seal from Karyes, Mount Athos with multiple lambs.

as stars, additional Crosses, flowers, rays, or other ornamentation. While the exact design of eucharistic seals varies, the basic elements remain consistent: a central Cross surrounded by the letters IC XC NI KA. Saint Symeon of Thessaloniki stresses that the square shape of the leavened Lamb is important, and differentiated from incorrect Roman Catholic practice, which uses a round unleavened Lamb.[9]

83

---

9. "The bread is four-sided, and not round and unleavened, as that sacrificed by the Latins, because as we said it is fully completed since God took on a fully complete human nature, with a soul and the four elements; and because all the world is four-part and the Word itself is the creator of the world; and because the body which Christ took on is made of four elements, and because the incarnate Word sanctified all the ends of the world, both the heavenly and the earthly, and because the shape of this typifies the cross, having been crucified and died on which, He restored us and the whole world." Saint Symeon of Thessaloniki, Περὶ τῆς ἱερᾶς λειτουργίας [On the Sacred Liturgy], in Ἡ Θεία εὐχαριστία. Εἰσηγήσεις, πορίσματα, ἱερατικοῦ συνέδριου τῆς ἱερᾶς μητροπόλεως Δράμας [The Divine Eucharist. Proceedings, conclusions of the priestly assembly of the Holy Metropolitan Diocese of Drama], ed. and modern Greek trans. Ioannes M. Fountoulis (Dramas, 2003), 194-371, par. 37.

Antidoron

The distribution of antidoron, for as long as it has been practiced in the Church, is another unifying act for the ecclesiastical community—something that is shared by all the gathered faithful following Holy Communion. Patriarch Theodore Balsamon of Alexandria suggested in the twelfth century that the Church, out of merciful loving kindness, offer blessed bread to those unable to receive the immaculate Mysteries. He also explains elsewhere that the distribution of antidoron at the end of the Divine Liturgy arose from a practical need to encourage worshipers to depart from the divine services in an orderly manner. This customary practice is unknown in the West.

Some archaeological findings raise questions about this practice in earlier centuries. Specifically, early seventh-century stamps have been discovered with the inscription, "the blessing of the Lord be upon us." Do such stamps, which were not used for prosphoro, give evidence that the distribution of antidoron occurred earlier than previously thought? Or were these stamps used in the general blessings that were described above? Some scholars believe that antidoron recalls the earlier practice of the "agape meal" from the early Church, while others believe that it was used to prepare "exorcism bread"—bread specifically given to catechumens as a blessing, since they were unable to receive Holy Communion. Whatever the case, we are certain that the distribution of blessed bread, taken from the eucharistic prosphoro, had become the prevailing practice by the ninth century.[10] The communal significance of antidoron is clear, since it was distributed to all Christians without distinction—both to communicants and non-communicants alike.

The prosphoro we bake in our homes and offer to the Church is of great significance. It allows us to participate in the mystery of the Church itself, the Body of Christ, and through our offering to partake in an earthly foretaste of the eternal joy of Paradise.

85

10.   The ancient Slavic practice was to distribute antidoron before the dismissal of the Divine Liturgy.

Everyday Stories

LET MY PRAYER RISE LIKE INCENSE BEFORE YOU

CHAPTER FIVE

The Prosphoro

By †Demetrios Stamati

It's a Saturday during Great Lent, and Orthros is about to begin. An old woman stands quietly at the candle stand in the narthex of her parish church. In her hands she holds a prosphoro that she has come to offer for the celebration of the Divine Liturgy.

She is modestly dressed in black, with a black scarf drawn low on her forehead framing a wrinkled but brightly shining face. Her countenance is sweet.

The prosphoro has been carefully wrapped with a clean white towel. On top of the prosphoro lays the woman's diptych—a piece of paper with the names of her loved ones, both living and reposed. In addition to her own family, the woman has written the names of her acquaintances who did not enjoy the blessing of children. There is a story from the life of Saint Makarios the Great of Egypt in which he tells of a certain occasion when he came upon the skull of an idolatrous priest in the desert. The great ascetic hears a voice come from the skull, saying, "Whenever you feel sorry for those who are in hell and pray for them, they receive a modicum of comfort." Perhaps the old woman had heard this story and was inspired to pray for her childless friends and acquaintances. Or perhaps she was familiar with what Saint John Chrysostom wrote concerning the importance of remembering the departed: "Not by accident did the holy Apostles decree that the departed should be commemorated in the presence of the awesome Mysteries. They knew there is much to be gained from that, much benefit."[1]

---

1. Saint John Chrysostom, as quoted in Hieromonk Gregorios, *The Divine Liturgy: A Commentary in the Light of the Fathers* (Columbia, Missouri: Newrome Press, 2020), 84.

There the old woman stood: clean, matronly, a humble parishioner. She is a portrait of solicitude, orderliness, and spiritual wisdom.

She has brought her prosphoro in good time, before the Service of Preparation has begun, unlike some who arrive just before the distribution of Holy Communion.

How wonderful it would be to watch her prepare prosphoro in her home, according to the old ways: with lit candle, an icon of the Panagia, and a small hand censer while softly chanting the Paraklesis.

There we would see the traditional kneading bowl, clean and set apart for its special purpose. The use of bread underlines the unity of the faithful, which is expressed in some early liturgical prayers, such as this one from the fourth century: "As this bread was scattered upon the mountains and was gathered and became one, do You likewise gather Your holy Church from every nation and every country and town and village and household and make one living Church."[2] The yeast is an image for the Kingdom of God that leavens

89

---

2. Ibid., 65.

the whole loaf.[3] The "whole loaf" here is the faithful gathered within the Church temple, being leavened all together, unified by the vigor of the Holy Spirit.

It is an inconceivable wonder how God receives these simple ingredients, taken from His creation, and with them brings about the union of God and man!

This is what I see: an "abbess" in the world, a simple-hearted woman living the mystery of man's union with God through the Divine Eucharist. The prosphoro that she has come to offer is her unique contribution to the realization of the union.

We, who count ourselves among the modern intellectual elite, give no thought to these things. We come to the Church empty-handed. We receive Holy Communion without having made even the slightest effort to bring the "first fruits of creation"; that is, the wheat, the wine, and the oil to the Church, which to us are forgotten customs. It is as if we imagine ourselves to be above such mundane concerns, and thus show ourselves to be blind fools.

The woman, whose mere presence in the church gladdens those present, delivers her prosphoro to one

---

3. Luke 13:18-21.

of the attendants at the candle stand. She prepared the bread with devotion and love according to Orthodox tradition. Now the prosphoro is given to the priest for the Service of Preparation, and in her heart she joins him in those mystical prayers. Everyone present shares in her joy. May God bless and justify her like He did the poor widow who cast "two small brass coins" (Luke 21:2) into the offering box in the Temple.[4]

---

4. This story originally appeared in *Anaplasis*, "The Parishioner," issue 373, Jan.-Feb. 1998.

Mrs. Christina

By Elisabeth Koulouri

My youthful years passed like a tempest.

Though my yiayia was a pious Orthodox Christian, prosphoro was not prepared in our home. As a young child I attended religious education classes at my local parish, like most young Greek girls in those days. In the six years that I attended those classes, I do not remember hearing the word *prosphoro*. When I turned fourteen, I became more attracted to a secular lifestyle and began to distance myself from the Church. My teenage mind imagined that Christ and joy were mutually exclusive.

However, like the Prodigal Son of the Gospel, there came a turning point in my life when I returned to the Church and her loving embrace. One day I met a priest, my future spiritual father, who reminded me that God is love and that Christ is the source of true joy. It was from this priest that I first heard about *leitouryiá*—liturgy bread, prosphoro—and how baking could truly be an expression of love. However, the process of preparing prosphoro seemed strange and tedious. What seemed most troublesome to me was that it required careful attention to small details and patience. I was accustomed to fast-food culture where everything was immediately available with little or no delay. However, if I was going to prepare prosphoro, I was expected to slow down, to wait for the dough to rise, and to carefully monitor the baking time to avoid over-browning the bread. I had always said that one day I would make prosphoro, but the truth was that I preferred to read a book about the history of prosphoro rather than to make it myself!

This is how I thought, until one day I was diagnosed with cancer, and required a lengthy course of chemotherapy. During my treatment, the Church became my life.

One day, in a small chapel off the beaten path, the church caretaker told me that someone had offered prosphoro on behalf of my healing. He told me that it had been prepared by an elderly woman named Mrs. Christina, and procceded to point her out to me. At that moment, the Service of Orthros was being celebrated and this woman was standing there like a statue, deep in prayer, gazing toward the holy Sanctuary. She was a person of medium height with a slight, even delicate, build. She was dressed in black with her white hair tied back—she had the brightest face, almost like that of a child. I was told that she was over eighty years old.

I was shocked by this news. Nothing like this had ever happened to me. A woman, completely unknown to me, had somehow learned of my illness and then went to the trouble of preparing prosphoro on my behalf.

From that day forward, this woman has had a place in my heart. On that occasion, we spoke only briefly after the Divine Liturgy. She had the habit of leaving church quickly, since she didn't drive and needed the assistance of another parishioner who would ferry her to and from church. I kept promising myself that I would visit her, but my "busyness" always prevented me from making the trip to her home. In truth, I neglected my obligation, and did not appreciate that people do not live forever.

Suddenly, in the middle of summer, Mrs. Christina passed away. I was heartbroken that I had not taken the time to visit her home, and to get to know her better. Someone who knew her well told me that she lived alone in a small house, because she never wanted to be a burden on her family. Apparently, her home was

immaculate and, though small in size, was most dig-
nified.

Mrs. Christina from Safika, the sister of a priest,
was a truly selfless person. In one of our very brief
conversations after divine services, she told me that
she had a pregnant daughter living in Crete at the
time. "I'm quite sick," she added, "but I don't want to
go to the hospital, because my daughter will want to
come to Athens and care for me. I'm afraid the stress
of the situation might endanger the baby."

After her death, Mrs. Christina was laid to rest in
the little cemetery of Makropoulo near the south wall.
Every time I pass the cemetery where she is buried I
remember something that I had once read, "In every
cemetery there are the relics of at least four or five
saints."

These events brought something to birth in me: the
strong desire to prepare prosphoro myself, and to offer it in the Church in memory of Mrs. Christina.

Noiselessly

By Dimitrios Stavrou

Margarita finished her lunch early. She arranged the space in the kitchen more hurriedly than usual. She went to the icon corner to retrieve the little oil lamp and hand censer, together with an icon of the Mother of God holding the Christ Child, and moved them to the kitchen table. Next she went to check on the yeast. She opened the container's lid and verified that the yeast looked healthy, and then placed the jar on the table. Then she tied her hair back, washed her hands carefully, and wiped down the table one final time.

Margarita made the Sign of the Cross and began to knead. "Lord Jesus Christ, have mercy on me." As she continued to knead she began to recall moments in her life beginning with her childhood in the countryside. She continued to knead the dough with slow, steady, patient movements. Her parents had died in a car accident while she was still in school, which forced her to grow up fast. "Lord Jesus Christ, have mercy on me." With her left hand she held the kneading bowl and with her right hand she continued to press the dough with her palm. She remembered the small house where she lived as a young woman, surrounded by books. Then she started working, until she finally met Andreas, the man who turned out to be her soulmate. Her mind returned to the task at hand. She was done kneading. "Lord Jesus Christ, have mercy on me." She sprinkled a little flour on the table.

Margarita had been married for six years. After three years, Andreas had begun to suffer from some kind of neurological disease. Initially the doctors thought that he had had a stroke. He stumbled over some words and began to walk with a limp. If only it were a stroke! "Most-holy Theotokos, save us!" Margarita took the dough out of the kneading bowl and began to shape it. Gradually Andreas' condition worsened. Eventually he lost control of his faculties and could no longer walk. Then there were intensive therapies, hospitalizations, physiotherapy, etc. A year and a half ago he could no longer speak, and it became increasingly difficult for him to write until that also became too difficult. "Most-holy Theotokos, save us!" The notebook that Andreas used to communicate with her was one of her most precious possessions. The dough-ball had become smooth, without a single

wrinkle or blemish. In time his breathing weakened and he required mechanical support. In the last few months of his life Andreas could only wink at her with his chestnut-colored eyes. In time his eyes closed and Margarita was even deprived of this last form of communication and expression of love. "Most-holy Theotokos, save us!"

She put the dough in the pan, made the Sign of the Cross with the wooden seal, and lay it on top of its perfectly smooth surface. "Holy Infant of Bethlehem, intercede for us!" With crossed hands she pressed the seal firmly into the dough. Then she carefully lifted the seal from the dough. She inspected the impression and saw the wondrous transformation of this earthly offering into something new: the dough had become prosphoro.

Margarita smiled to herself. "Holy one of God, first-called Apostle Andrew, intercede for us!" She was older now, slightly bent with age. Her hair had begun to turn gray and she always kept her reading glasses at the ready. She was an inconspicuous presence in the neighborhood and a nearly silent fixture in her parish. "Holy Martyr of God, Margarita, intercede for us!" While waiting for the prosphoro to rise, she read the

Paraklesis to the Mother of God. She read the words slowly and carefully, not wanting to miss a single syllable. She concluded with a little prayer.

She placed the pan with the prosphoro in the preheated oven. Then she began to prepare the table. She laid out white embroidered towels for the prosphoro. Next, she began to write her commemoration list. On one piece of paper she wrote the names of the living, and on another piece of paper she wrote the names of those who had fallen asleep in the Lord. She was careful to write each name legibly. As she wrote each name she offered a prayer. The past has passed. "Lord Jesus Christ, have mercy on me." And what is now has already passed—even as each word is formed with the tongue, it vanishes into the fog of history. "Most Holy Theotokos, save us!" The future is our only hope. "Holy Saints of God, intercede for us!"

Margarita removes the pan from the oven and upturns it over one of the embroidered towels. She moves in a quiet rhythm. First she combs her hair, then closes the windows, puts on her shoes, and washes her hands. She removes the prosphoro from the first towel and wraps it in the second so that it doesn't become ruined from moisture. Then she places the towel-wrapped prosphoro in a cloth bag together with her commemoration lists. She closes the front door and locks it with her key. The bolt clunks shut. Silence. She makes her way to the church for Vespers where she will present her offering together with her names. "I look for the resurrection of the dead, and the life of the age to come. Amen."

Photographic Aids

Traditional Starter

Bread flour

Spring water

Fresh basil

Two indications of a healthy starter are the presence of
bubbles of varying sizes, and a slightly acidic odor.

Prep and Baking Needs

High-sided baking pan

Pastry brush, beeswax, kitchen towel

Digital scale

Rolling pin

Kneading Aids

Bear Dough Mixer
Available in two sizes, 5L / 7L with a suggested
Artisan Bread Flour max capacity of 1600 gr / 2200 gr, respectively.

Kitchenaid Mixer
The suggested max capacity for the
4.5 qt model (shown) is 1152 gr of
Artisan Bread Flour.

Thermomix TM6
The suggested max capacity is
800 gr of Artisan Bread Flour.

Kneading and Rest Periods

Dough after 30 minute autolysis.

Kneading after 30 minute autolysis.

Kneading after first 10 minute rest.

Kneading after second 10 minute rest.

Kneading after third 10 minute rest. Notice smooth texture of the dough.

Properly measured, prepared, and rested prosphoro dough will not stick to your fingers.

Shaping, Stamping, Baking, and Steaming

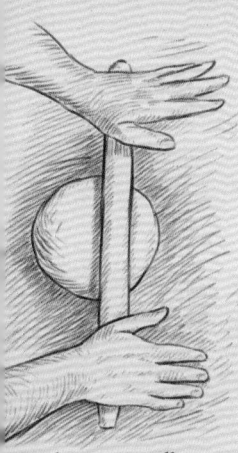

Start by using a rolling pin to flatten the dough.

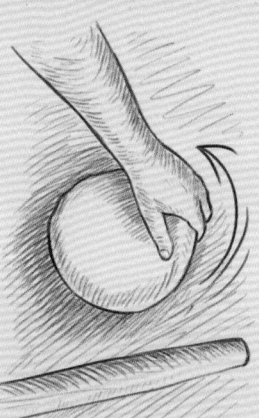

Rotate the dough counter-clockwise 45 degrees and roll again.

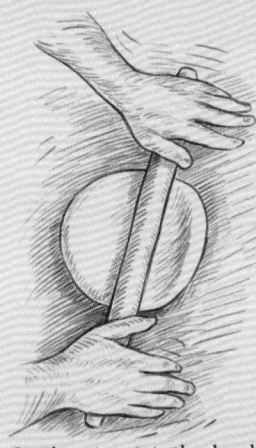

Continue to rotate the dough; smooth and flatten with the rolling pin.

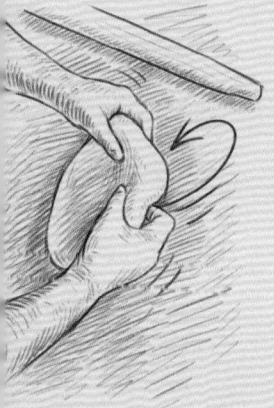

Next, flip the dough and begin shape the dough into a ball.

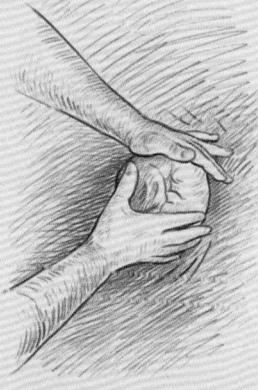

Gather the edges of the dough and draw them up into itself.

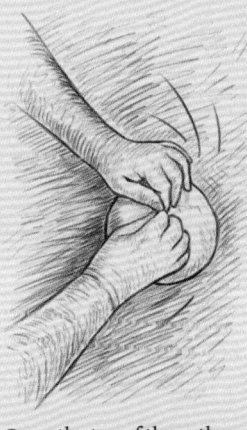

Press the top of the gathered edges into the dough and press down.

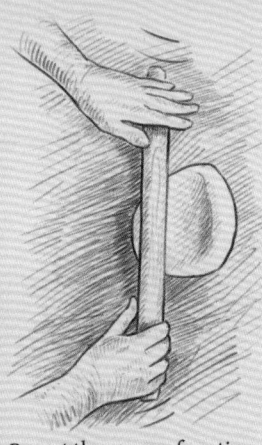

Repeat the process four times. Use less pressure with the rolling pin each time you repeat these steps.

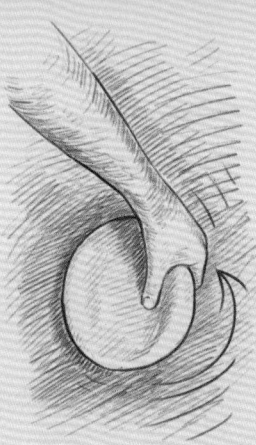

Rotate the dough counter-clockwise 45 degrees.

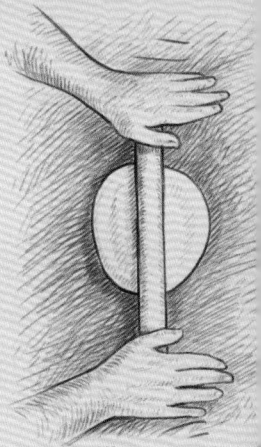

Use the rolling pin to smooth and flatten. Then rotate and repeat.

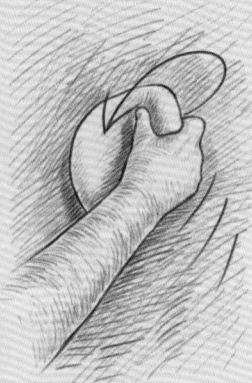

Flip the dough again and shape the dough into a ball.

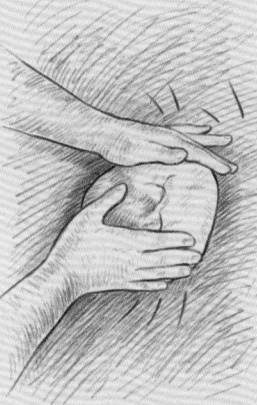

Gather the edges of the dough and draw them up into itself.

Press the top of the gathered edges into the dough and press down.

As you repeat this process, the dough will become smoother and the ball shape will improve.

Finally press down on
the ball of dough.

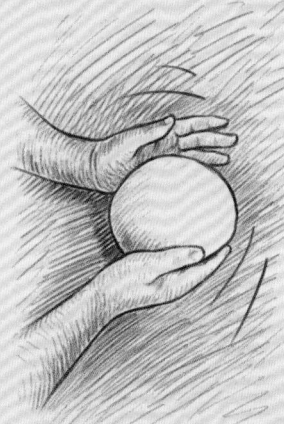

Then, while rotating the dough ball
between your palms, press the edges
of the dough under the ball. Continue
until you get the desired shape.

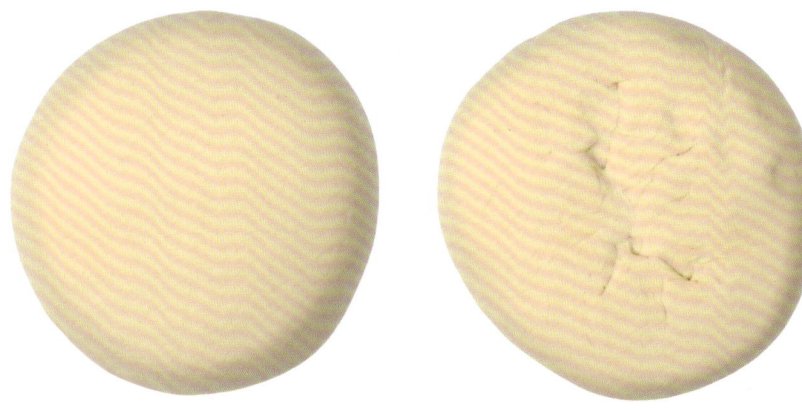

After shaping, top of loaf.   *After shaping, bottom of loaf.*

Shaped loaf in pan, before 15 minute stamping rest.

Shaped loaf in pan, after 15 minute stamping rest.

16cm, hand-carved prosphoro seal from Mount Athos.
Available for purchase from monastiriaka.gr

Prosphoro, after applying the pictured 16 cm stamp
in 8-inch high-sided pan.

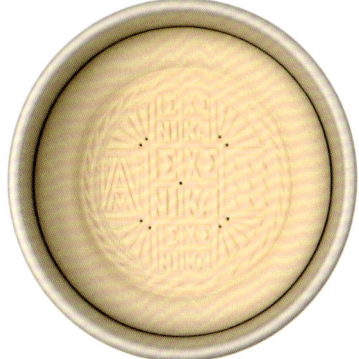

The prosphoro may be pierced if desired, though it is not necessary.

There are many possible piercing patterns.

State of rise after 2 hours.

State of rise after 4 hours.

State of rise after 6 hours. *State of rise after 8 hours.*

Prosphoro after 55 minute bake.*

* Note the slightly darker coloration at the top right. This can happen if the oven cavity has hot spots, or if the foil covering was put in place too late during baking.

*Cooled
prosphoro.*

Steam-glazed prosphora.

Artoclasia
Kneading, Rest Periods, Shaping,
amd Other Necessities

Kneading after 30 minute autolysis.

Kneading after first 10 minute rest.

Kneading after second 10 minute rest.

Kneading after third 10 minute rest.

Artoclasia after being pressed into the pan.

Artoclasia after the application of seasame seeds.

Artoclasia after baking.

Detail of Artoclasia.

Other required items for the
celebration of the Service of Artoclasia

Wheat berries.

Wine for Holy Communion.

Olive Oil.

Five beeswax tapers.

Helpful Hints

Seals that lack definition will produce less desirable results.

*Hand carved antique seal.**

A seal that lacks definition will pro-
duce a faint impression.

Seals with deep engravings,
as pictured above, produce the best results.

* *The antique seal pictured was loaned to the editor for testing purposes.*

*Perimeter tearing
is evidence of under-rising.*

*Poor seal definition
is evidence of over-rising.*

*Seal tearing / cracking is
evidence of under-rising.*

*Seal deformation
is evidence of over-rising.*

A sunken seal is evidence of over-rising,
while dark coloration and webbed sur-
face cracks are signs of over-baking.